You Can Teach Yourself® JAZZ PIANO

By Uri Ayn Rovner

FOREWORD

Welcome to the world of *jazz piano!* You've been enjoying the piano and for a long time enjoying the sounds of jazz. Well, you've come to the right place to dig in! There's an adventure in sound ahead for you and your keyboard.

This book is divided into three sections:

The *WORKBOOK* comes first. Since you know your basic music notation and some theory already, you will find this just the thing to take you deeper into what makes this exciting music tick. You'll be improvising, analyzing, and writing your own music before you know it! (Also in this series: *YOU CAN TEACH YOURSELF® PIANO*.)

The *FAKEBOOK* lets you read from lead charts just like the pros. These charts are in alphabetical order, not level of difficulty. Experiment with accompaniment styles, chord voicings, and melody enhancing. All of your own design!

The *SONGBOOK* is a collection of 27 songs in a variety of jazz styles. (Hopefully some of your favorite styles!) They are presented with the easiest first progressing to the more advanced. You don't have to play them in order though, and you'll enjoy skipping around.

YOU CAN TEACH YOURSELF® JAZZ PIANO will prepare you for more advanced jazz piano study. You'll know what jazz is all about, and feel right at home with its sound. If you fancy blues, check out the book *YOU CAN TEACH YOURSELF® BLUES PIANO*. You'll soon discover new jazz artists, and can enjoy listening and playing their styles.

Uri Ayn Rovner

A recording of the music in this book is now available. The publisher strongly recommends the use of this recording along with the text to insure accuracy of interpretation and ease in learning.

© 1998 BY MEL BAY PUBLICATIONS, INC., PACIFIC, MO 63069.
ALL RIGHTS RESERVED. INTERNATIONAL COPYRIGHT SECURED. B.M.I. MADE AND PRINTED IN U.S.A.

Visit us on the Web at http://www.melbay.com — E-mail us at email@melbay.com

CONTENTS

WORKBOOK

CHAPTER 1 – TRIADS 4
    I and V chords 7   Inversions 11
    ALL FOR ONE 9   Twelve Bar 13
    Key Signatures 10   Minor Chords 14

CHAPTER 2 – EXTEND THOSE CHORDS 16
    Dominant Seventh Chords 16   Creating **LIGHT BLUE** 23
    Other Seventh Chords 18   Ninth Chords 24
    Dominant Qualities 19   Thirteenth Chords 25
    YOUR SONG 21   Diminished & Augmented Chords 27
    Blue Notes 22   Chord Symbols 29

CHAPTER 3 – OTHER VOICINGS 30
    Chords in Fourths 30   Left Hand Voicings 35
    APPLE BETTY 33   **FAR AWAY PLACES** 38

CHAPTER 4 – MODES AND SUCH 40
    The Seven Modes 40   **VERNA** 47
    Matching Chords 43   Blues Scale 49
    Using Modes 45   **HIGHWAY ONE, DETOUR!** 51
    OH, WHEN THE SAINTS 46   Manuscript Paper 52

  How to Swing 66

FAKEBOOK
  Accompaniment Patterns 54
  Getting Started 56
    Anywhere 57
    Apple Betty 58
    Fiero 59
    Flap Jacks 59
    Inch O'Blues 60
    Jambo 60
    Kiss Me 61
    Namorada 62
    Pop Quiz 62
    Quarter Of 63
    St. James Infirmary 64
    You Basket 64
    Zambezi 65

SONGBOOK
    Sesame Rag 68
    Highway 1 69
    Miss Turee 70
    Something Doing, by Scott Joplin & Scott Haydn 71
    Kaplooey Louey 72
    1 2 3 74
    Flap Jacks 76
    Elite Syncopations, by Scott Joplin 77
    Sally Mander 78
    Borneo Bay 80
    Powder Room Rag 82
    Choc'late Cake 84
    Hong Kong Farewell 86
    Moonlight In Your Eyes 88
    Last Train To Edison 90
    Hesitating Blues, by W.C. Handy 92
    Just Like Before 93
    Manitoulin 95
    Slap Jack 96
    Fiver 98
    The Happy Dee Homemaker Show 100
    Maraca 103
    You're Wrong (Piano Solo) 106
    You're Wrong (Piano/Vocal) 109
    Fiesta 113
    Blues Montgomery 116
    Fender Bender 118

WORKBOOK

CHAPTER 1 — TRIADS

Chords are the words of music. If you want to make up your own music, or understand the music you read and hear, you will need to know chords and their use. A dictionary of the basic three note chords (triads), along with their structure and use are found in this chapter. It is important to have a handle on these chords before continuing on to the next lessons.

When ROOT POSITION chords are written, the three notes are all on lines or all on spaces. The chord's name is the bottom note. It looks like a "snowman"!

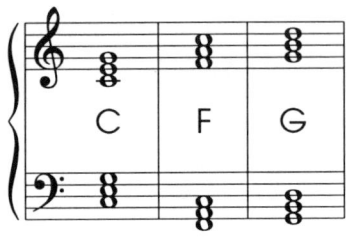

The distance between the notes is not exactly the same. Notice the INTERVAL OF A THIRD between the bottom notes is larger than the third between the top

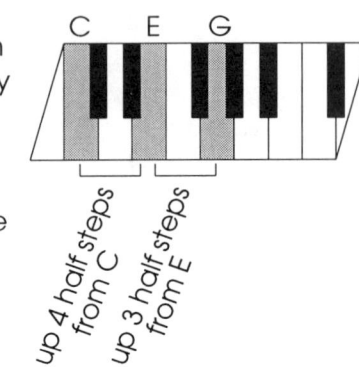

To keep the same interval relationship, in many chords sharps or flats are needed.

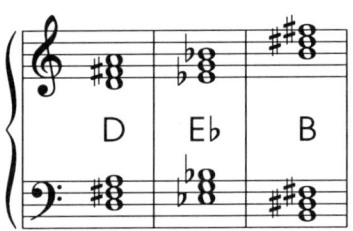

HERE ARE ALL TWELVE ROOT POSITION TRIADS SHOWN IN CHROMATIC ORDER STARTING WITH THE "C" CHORD. PLAY THEM AS YOU READ THEM.

PLAYED   WRITTEN

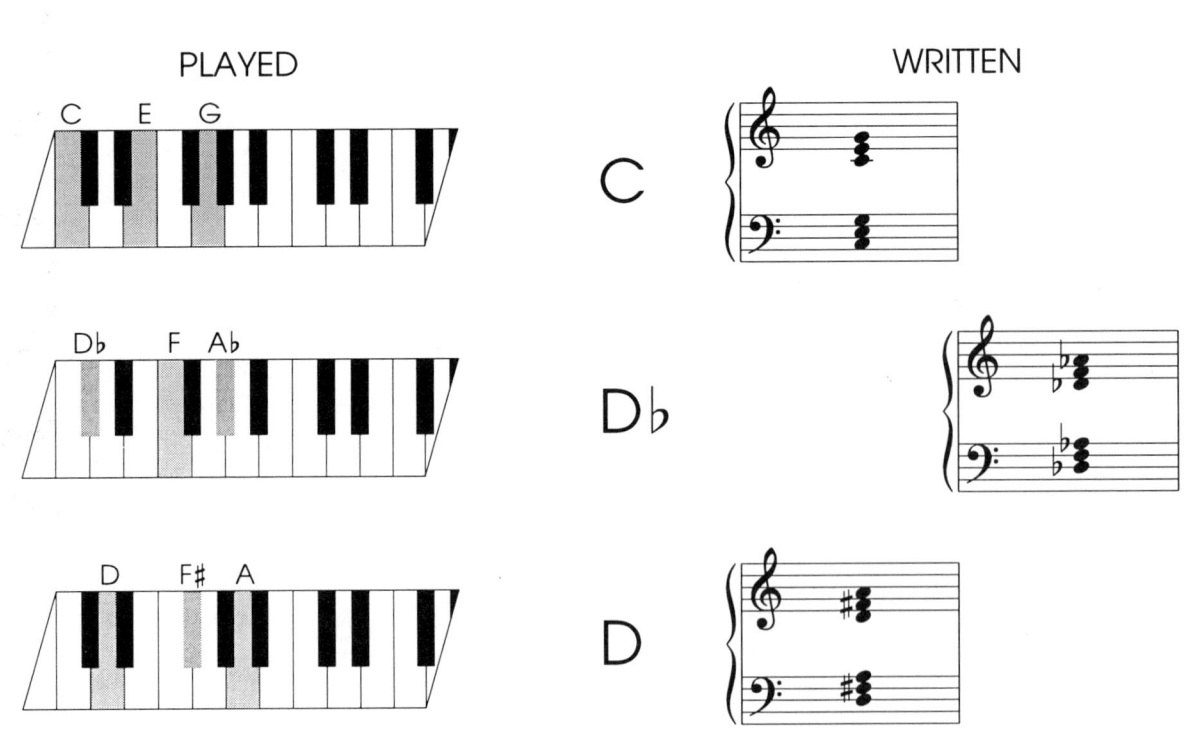

4

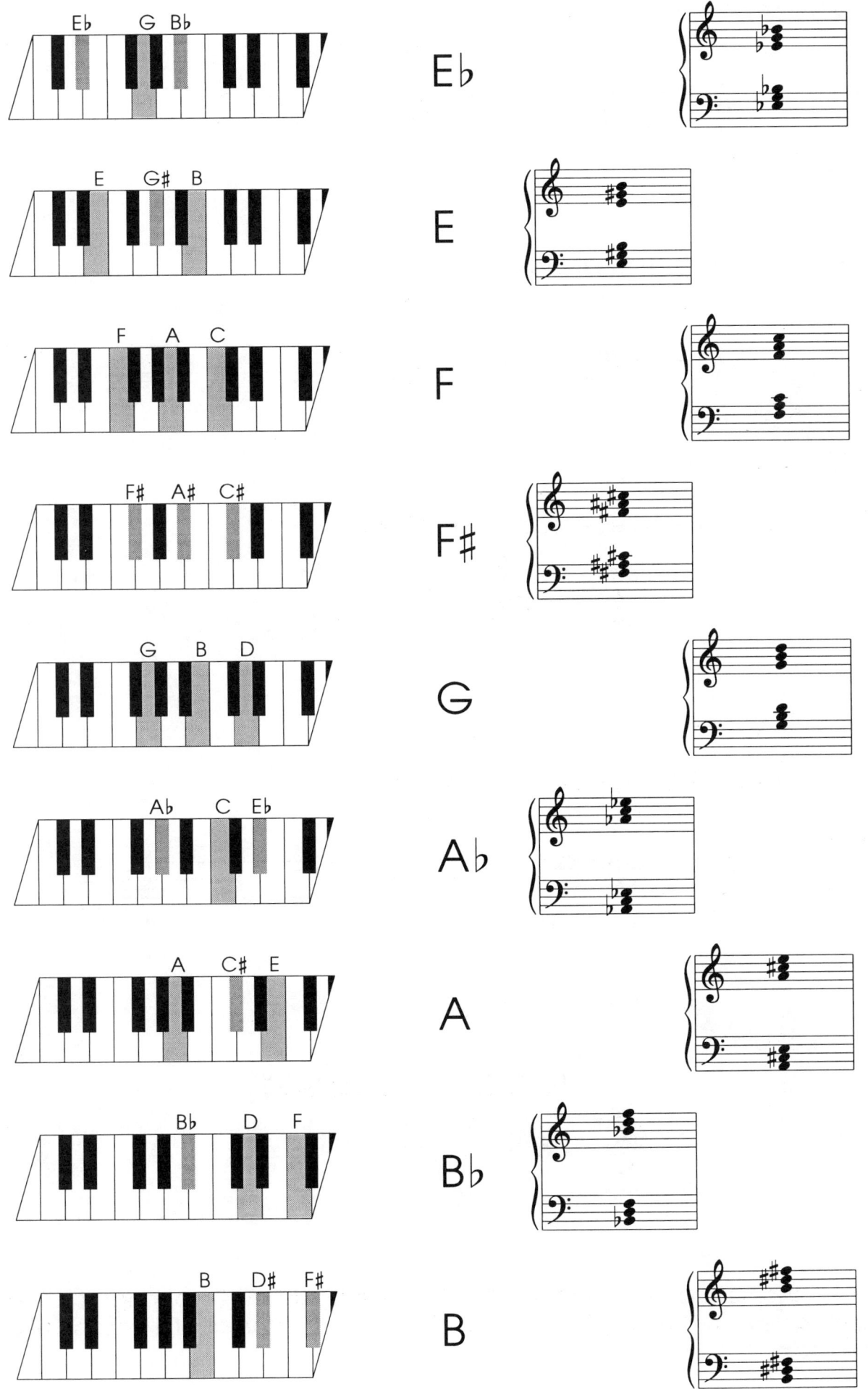

Three chords use only white notes:

Three need a black note in the middle:

"B" is busy with two black notes — and "B♭" is not busy:

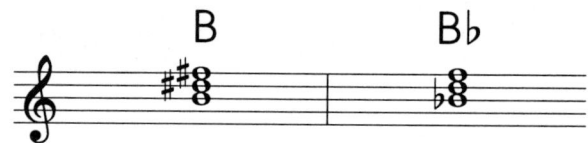

Three chords need a white note only in the middle:

One chord is all black:

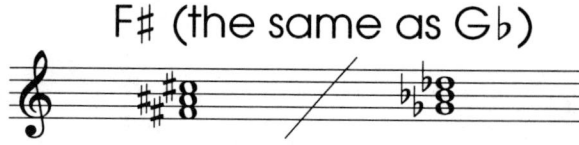

Any of these chords can be the leader chord or "HOME CHORD" in a song. If "C" is home note in a song, we say the song is in the "KEY OF C". All the chords of that song relate to the home chord.

THE I AND V CHORDS

Let's say that C is home, or I (one in Roman numerals). This implies that the whole C chord is "HOME CHORD". A complete song has at least two different chords. The next most important chord is called the DOMINANT or V (five in Roman numerals). It is the *interval of a fifth* higher than home note.

The top of the I chord is the name of the V chord.
If C is I then G is V.

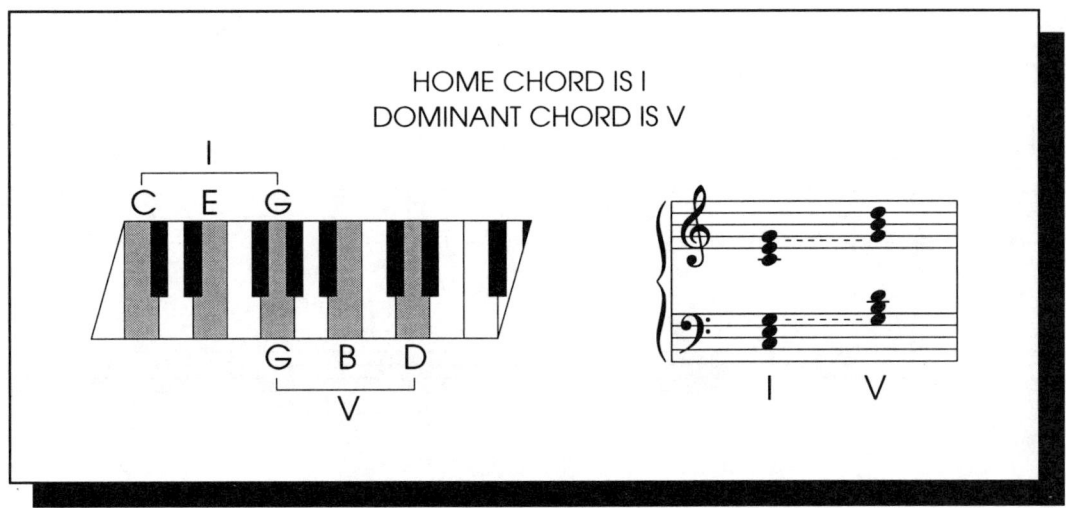

Place your LH (left hand) on a C chord.
Now put your pinky where your thumb is.
Your hand will move up to the G or V chord.

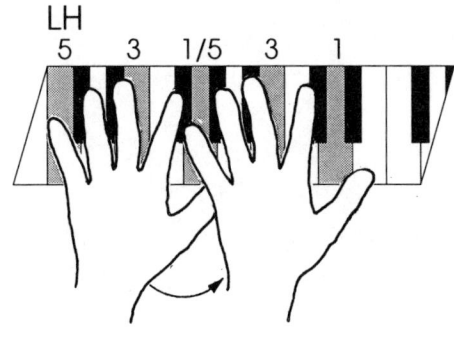
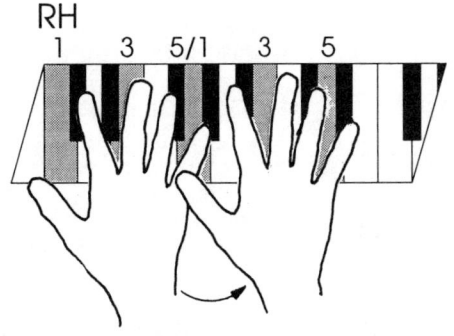

To move your RH (right hand) to a V chord,
move your thumb to where your pinky is.

You can now create a song with the formula: I V I.

Place both hands on C chords an octave apart. A good placement for the LH would be the octave below middle C. The LH will play the chord BLOCKED (all notes at the same time), and the RH will play notes in the C chord one at a time in any pattern.

Then both hands will move up to the V chord and continue in the same way. Finish your song by going back to the I chord. Songs like to end at home!

example song: I V I in C

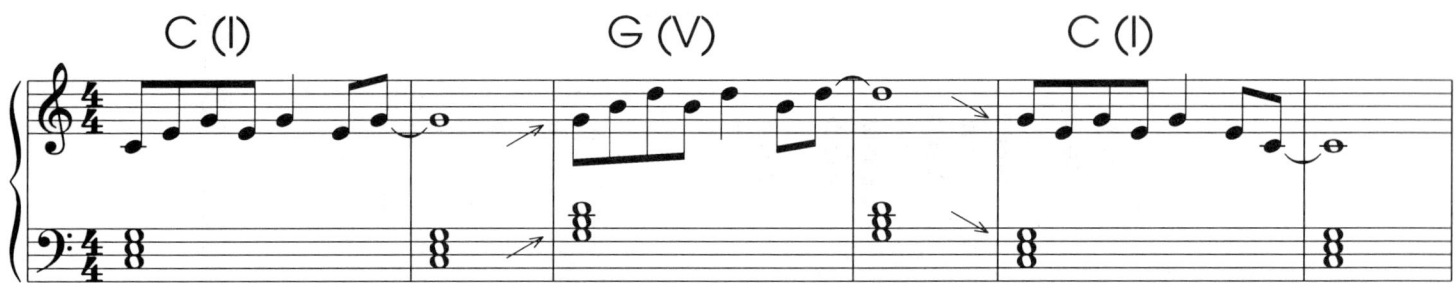

Can you play the example song in another key? Try starting with both hands on a G chord. Read the same pattern in the first two measures. Then move both hands up to the V chord, which is D. (Don't forget to use the F# in the middle.) After measures three and four, move back down to the I chord to finish. You have now TRANSPOSED this song to the key of G!

Can you transpose it to another key?

Improvise your own melody in the RH over the I V I chords. Then try to remember what you played. Then, for fun you can transpose it to another key! Soon you will find other LH patterns to play, and become creative with your melodies.

THE IV CHORD

The next most important chord in a song is the SUB-DOMINANT. It's called the IV chord (4 in Roman numerals), and is found by moving *one whole step (two individual notes) lower* than the V chord. It is called sub-dominant because it is also V *below* home.

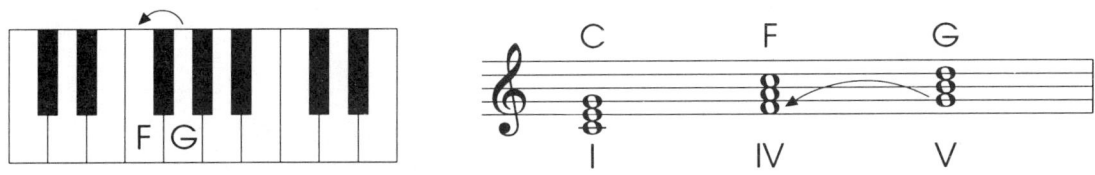

Listen to these three chords several times. Which one sounds like home to you? Will it make a good ending chord for a song?

I IV V in F

In this example of a song using I IV and V in F, notice how the LH rhythm enhances the melody. In the melody, chordal notes are used, but not always in root position. Will that sound O.K.? A few chords seem to be missing, go ahead and write them in!

ALL FOR ONE

* Non-chordal tone

© 1998 BY MEL BAY PUBLICATIONS, INC., PACIFIC, MO 63069.
ALL RIGHTS RESERVED. INTERNATIONAL COPYRIGHT SECURED. B.M.I.

KEY SIGNATURES

Below is a list of the I IV V chords for all 12 keys. A KEY SIGNATURE is the number of sharps or flats used in the three primary chords or any key. This is written at the beginning of the line in music so that you'll remember which ACCIDENTALS to use while you play. Also use this list to improvise with the correct notes in your song!

Key	I	IV	V	Key Signature		Key	I	IV	V	Key Signature
C	C	F	G	(no sharps/flats)		F	F	Bb	C	1 flat
G	G	C	D	1 sharp		Bb	Bb	Eb	F	2 flats
D	D	G	A	2 sharps		Eb	Eb	Ab	Bb	3 flats
A	A	D	E	3 sharps		Ab	Ab	Db	Eb	4 flats
E	E	A	B	4 sharps		Db	Db	Gb	Ab	5 flats
B	B	E	F#	5 sharps		Gb	Gb	Cb	Db	6 flats

10

INVERSIONS

Chords have other positions besides root position. These are called INVERSIONS. Sometimes an inversion is more convenient to reach with your hand as you move from chord to chord. Because the same three notes are in the chord, it has the same function as the root chord. Inversions add a different "color" to the chord's sound. These are two basic inversions.

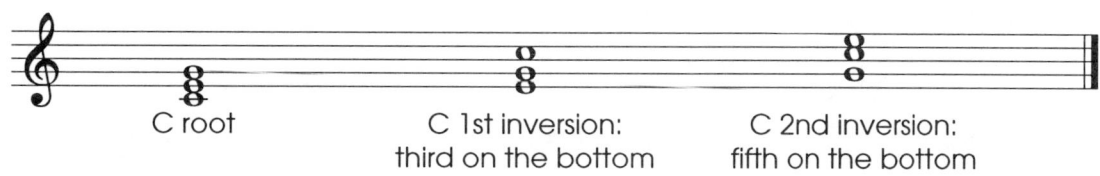

C root   C 1st inversion: third on the bottom   C 2nd inversion: fifth on the bottom

ALL CHORDS HAVE INVERSIONS, HERE ARE SOME EXAMPLES
Some seem to be missing! Can you fill them in?

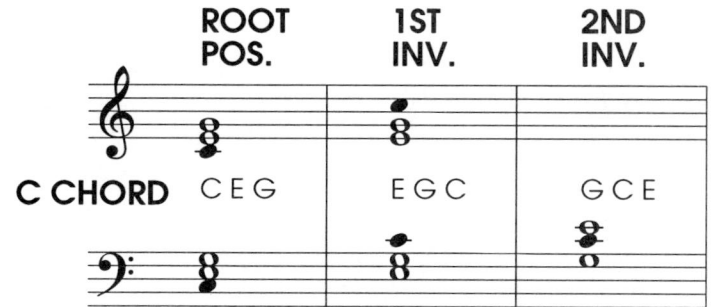

C CHORD   C E G   E G C   G C E

B CHORD   B D# F#   D# F# B   F# B D#

D CHORD   D F# A   F# A D   A D F#

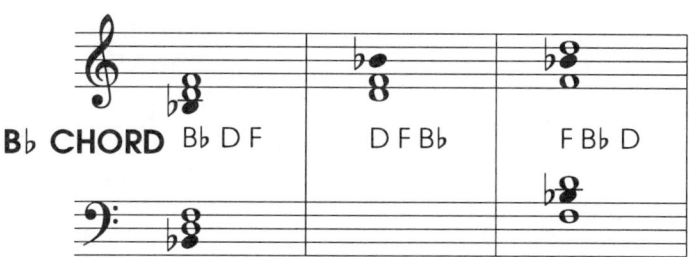

Bb CHORD   Bb D F   D F Bb   F Bb D

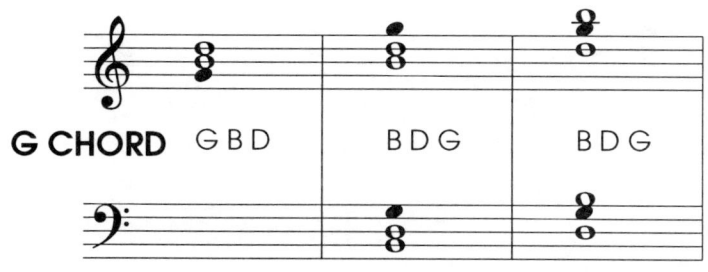

G CHORD   G B D   B D G   B D G

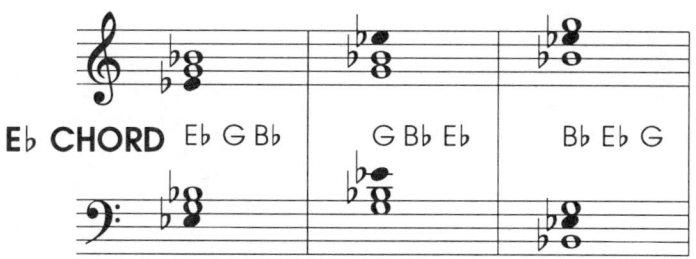

Eb CHORD   Eb G Bb   G Bb Eb   Bb Eb G

These are standard fingerings for chord inversions. However, use whatever fingering works best for you when reading or improvising.

What fingerings would you use for these examples?

Here are some examples of inversions as they appear in songs from this book:

FIESTA

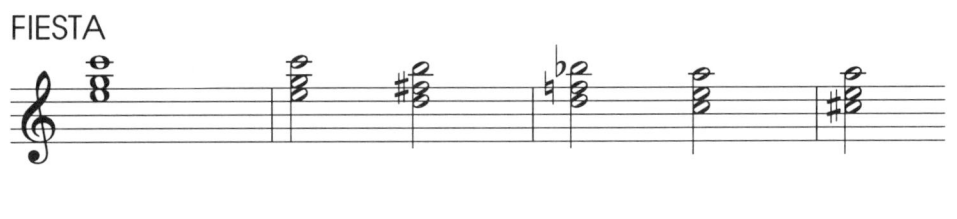

ELITE SYNCOPATIONS

POWDER ROOM RAG

TWELVE BAR

A pattern of chords often heard in jazz songs is a TWELVE BAR. This twelve measure pattern uses the following chords:

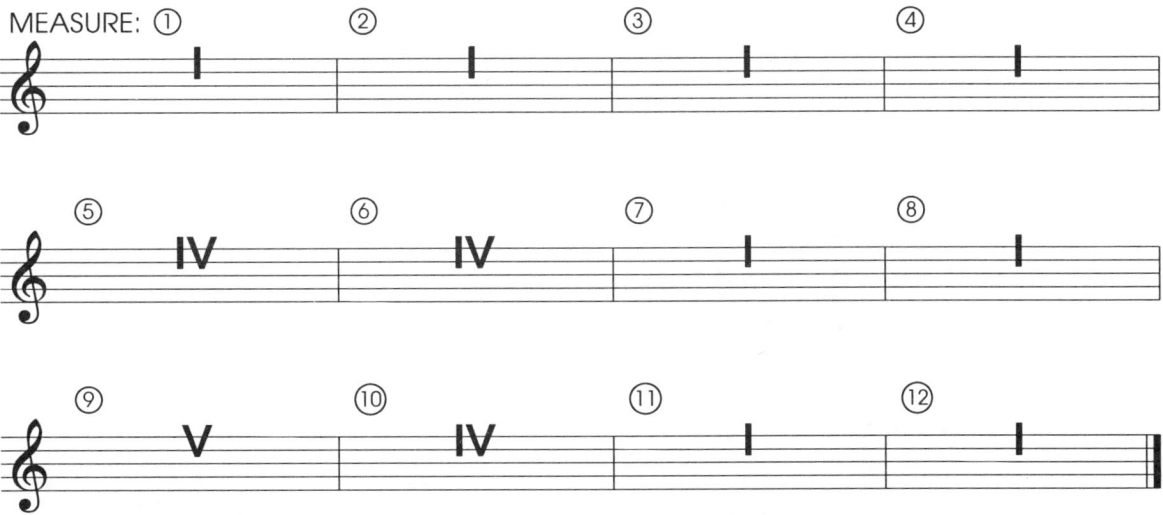

You will find this twelve bar pattern, or a variation of it (pg. 51), in the following songs:

> Highway 1 Pop quiz
> Inch O' Blues Hesitating Blues
> Borneo Bay Manitoulin

CREATING A TWELVE BAR SONG

Follow these six steps to create your own song. Improvise to practice, and then write out your song. You'll find some blank manuscript on pg. 52.

1. Decide on a key for your song.
2. Choose a left hand pattern (see pp. 54 & 55), and see how it works for the I, IV, and V chords.
3. Create a melody for the first line:
   A. A 2 measure idea (or riff), repeated, to make the first 4 measures. Try a long note or rest at the end.
   B. A 4 measure idea with a long note or rest at the end.
4. Play the same or similar melody for the second line (measures 5 - 8). The same pattern can be adjusted to the IV chord notes.
5. For the V IV measures (9 & 10), create something different. Repeat the last two measures of another line for the end.
6. Decide on finishing touches: tempo, dynamics, which octave played in, swing (pg. 66), etc.

MINOR CHORDS

The chords we have been working with are called MAJOR chords. MINOR chords are different than major chords. The third of the chord is lowered a half step.

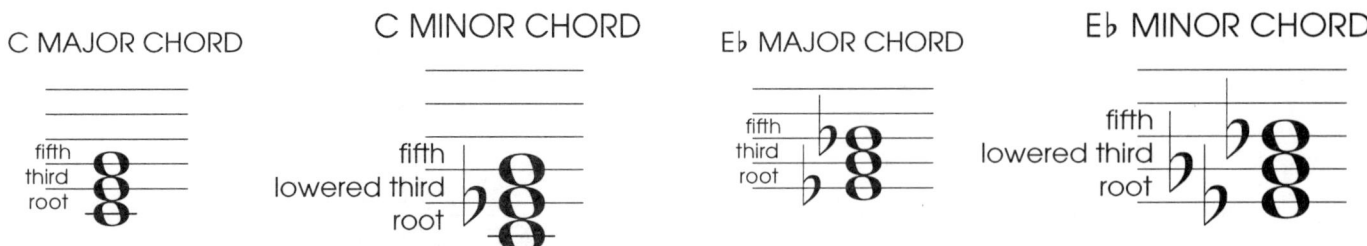

Any minor chord can be home chord. For instance, a song can be in the key of C minor. In this case, the primary chords of the song would be: <u>i iv v</u>. All three chords would be minor. Home chords, however, even when minor, sound best with a major V chord. So, most often a song in a minor key has <u>i iv V</u> for primary chords.

<u>In this book, the following songs are in a minor key</u>:

Miss Turee   **Zambezi**   **St. James Infirmary**   **Fiesta**

Minor chords are also used in songs with a major I chord. They are usually chords that are not I IV or V. Most often this minor chord will be a fifth higher than the V chord. This minor chord is called the ii chord.

If C is home, then:

This phrase is in the key of C. Can you label these chords by name and function number?:

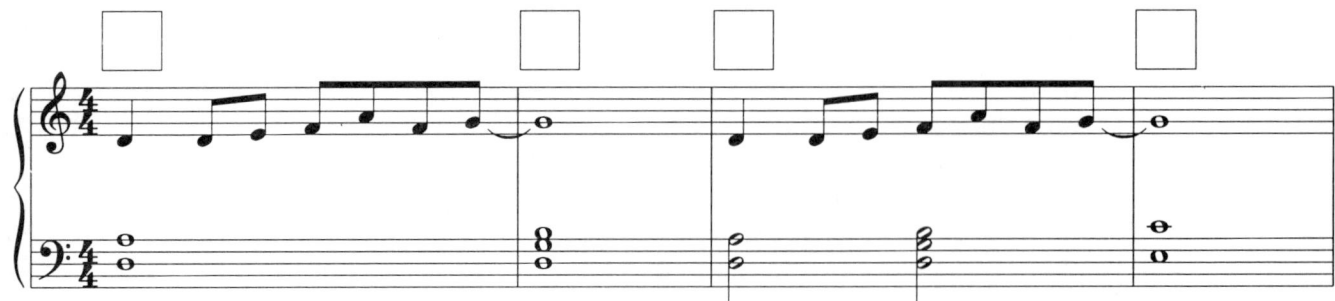

It goes further than this! If we continue this "fives" game, we could use the chord five above the ii chord. This would be the vi chord. Five above the vi chord is the iii chord.

Notice why five above the V chord is called ii. It is named ii because it is based on the second step of the scale in any key. The five of ii is called vi because it is a chord based on the sixth step of the scale. Go up a fifth from vi and you will be on the third step of the scale, or iii.

Find the ii, vi & iii chords for the following keys:

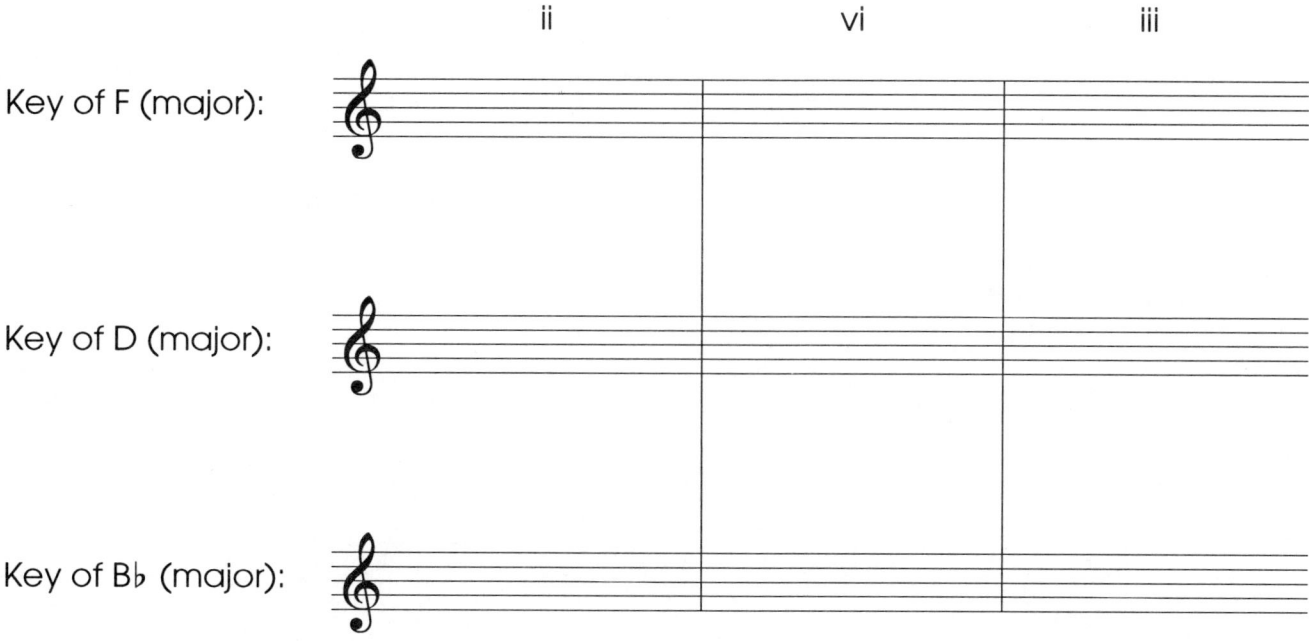

A common progression in jazz is: ii V ii V ii V, etc. This is often heard when a solo is being improvised above it. You may even see the ii chord played as a major chord (then labelled II chord). There is always the danger of the V chord sounding like home in that case. Sometimes that's just what you want!

CHAPTER 2   EXTEND THOSE CHORDS!

DOMINANT 7TH CHORDS

The note most commonly added to a triad is the 7th (seventh). Our "snowman" will now add another third on top. The distance from the bottom to the top of this four note chord is called the INTERVAL OF A SEVENTH. It is important that this note on top is one WHOLE STEP LOWER than the name of the chord.

For a G chord this would be an F: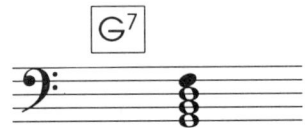

For a C chord this would be a B♭: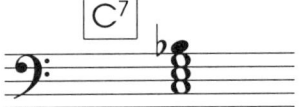

For an A♭ chord this would be a G♭:

Can you write the sevenths on top of the following chords?:

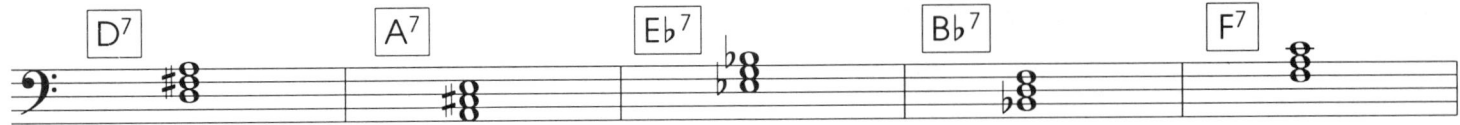

A chord with a 7th in it will function like a V chord with a IV chord note added to it. This chord has a very active sound because it tends to pull your ear down a fifth to the home chord. Even home chord can add a seventh if it wants to lead your ear to the chord down a fifth.

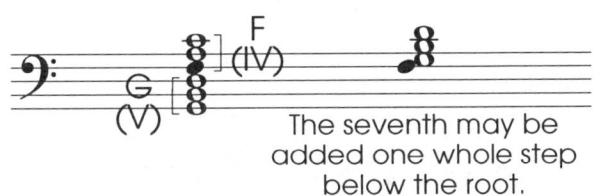

The seventh may be added one whole step below the root.

Some possible voicings for all 12:
DOMINANT SEVENTH CHORDS

OTHER SEVENTH CHORDS

Some chords, home chord for instance, may not want to sound active in some styles or songs. Not wanting to feel that drive to go down a fifth, these chords add a MAJOR SEVENTH instead. A major seventh is only a HALF STEP lower than the root of the chord. It creates a larger interval from the bottom of the "snowman" to the top than a dominant seventh.

Major seventh chord example:

Minor chords can have sevenths. A ii chord is minor, and acts as five above the V chord.

Minor seventh chord example:

If a minor chord is home, it may sound nice with a major seventh.

Minor major seventh chord:

<u>Here are some cuts from songs in this book. Can you name the seventh chords?</u>

from:
"Fiesta"

"Just Like Before"

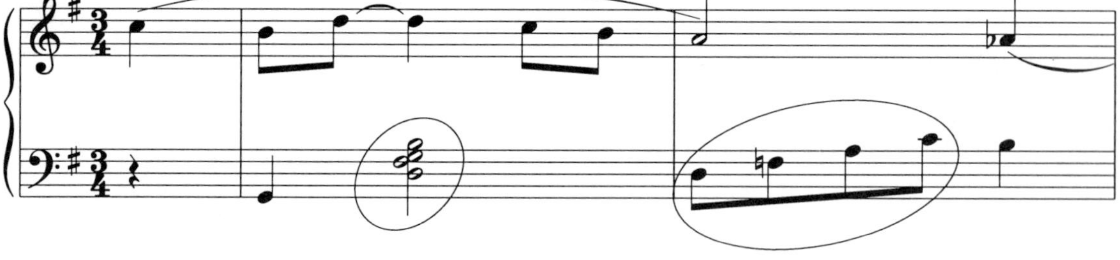

"Choc'late Cake"

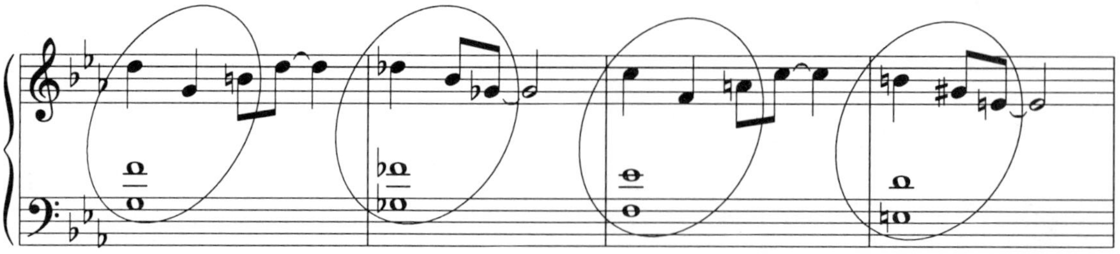

18

DOMINANT QUALITIES

Any chord moving down a fifth creates a stronger sounding chord. That is why the progression V - I can create a home chord sound. A major chord creates a stronger progression down a fifth. Add a seventh to a minor or major chord before going down, to create an even stronger stability.

Play and listen to the following examples. Can you hear any difference in the way the C chords function when different qualities of chords precede them?

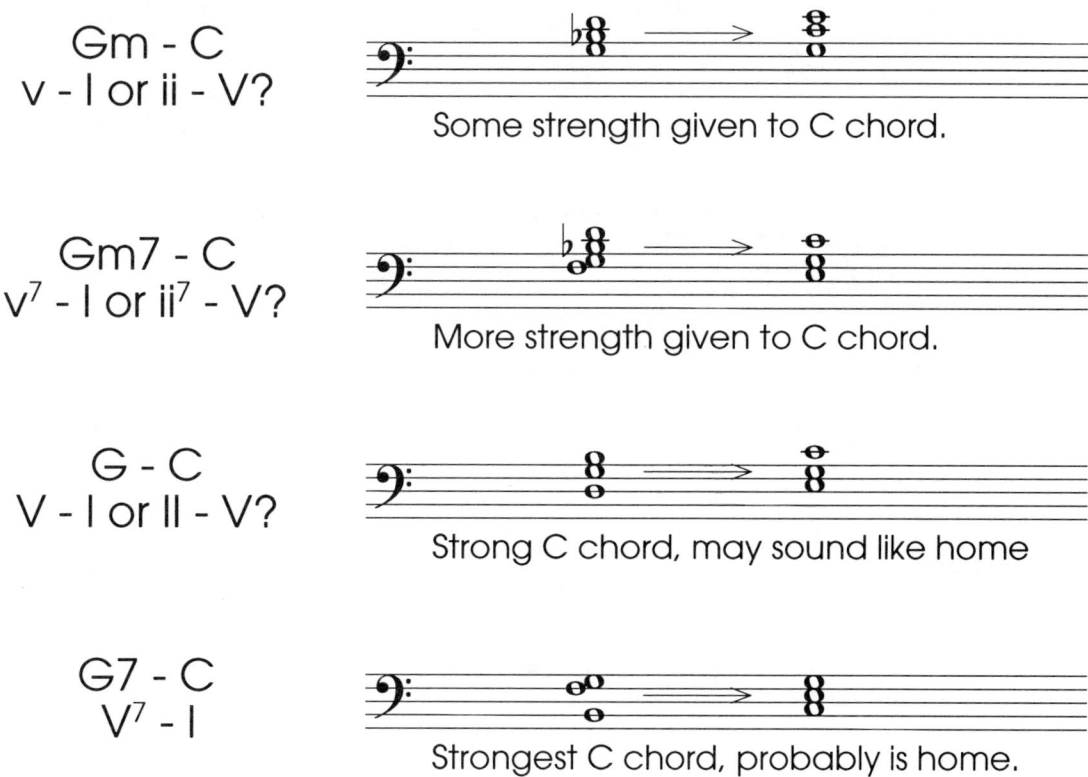

Gm - C
v - I or ii - V?
Some strength given to C chord.

Gm7 - C
v7 - I or ii7 - V?
More strength given to C chord.

G - C
V - I or II - V?
Strong C chord, may sound like home

G7 - C
V7 - I
Strongest C chord, probably is home.

CHECK THIS OUT:

In ex. 2, what would happen if a 7th were added to the C chord?

What if you wanted to change to the key of F! You will have to continue down another fifth. How will you arrange the chord qualities above to get from G - C - F? Listen to your choices to hear how strong the F chord is. Does it sound like home?

In the last example, if you precede the G7 with a II chord, should it be major or minor? Should it have a seventh? Why? What chord could precede the II chord?

The four notes of a 7th chord will be used in melody making as well. Melodies may be created from short musical ideas, or RIFFS. These can be repeated or developed into musical PHRASES creating a melody. Note the examples, then try your hand at writing some riffs. Use only the four notes from the chord and hear how creative you can be! (Play your riffs over a blocked left hand chord.)

Examples:

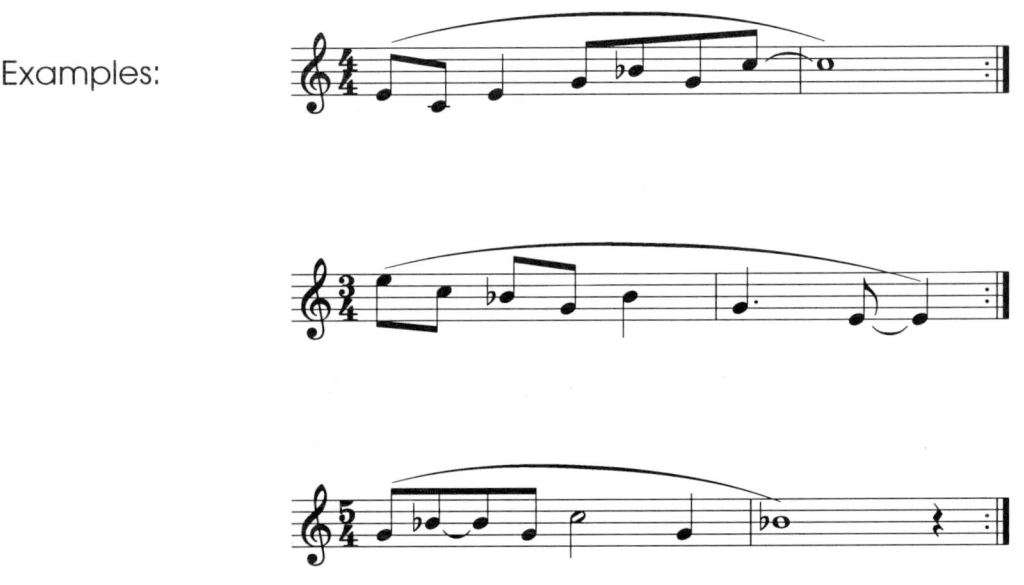

Try writing a few of your own:

Use one of your riff ideas from pg. 20 to create a melody over this walking bass.

song title: _____

how to be played: _____   your name: _____

BLUE NOTES

BLUE NOTES are a popular item in jazz, and especially in the BLUES style. These notes occur in the melody. The third of a major chord is played a half step lower, and then slides up to the regular third.

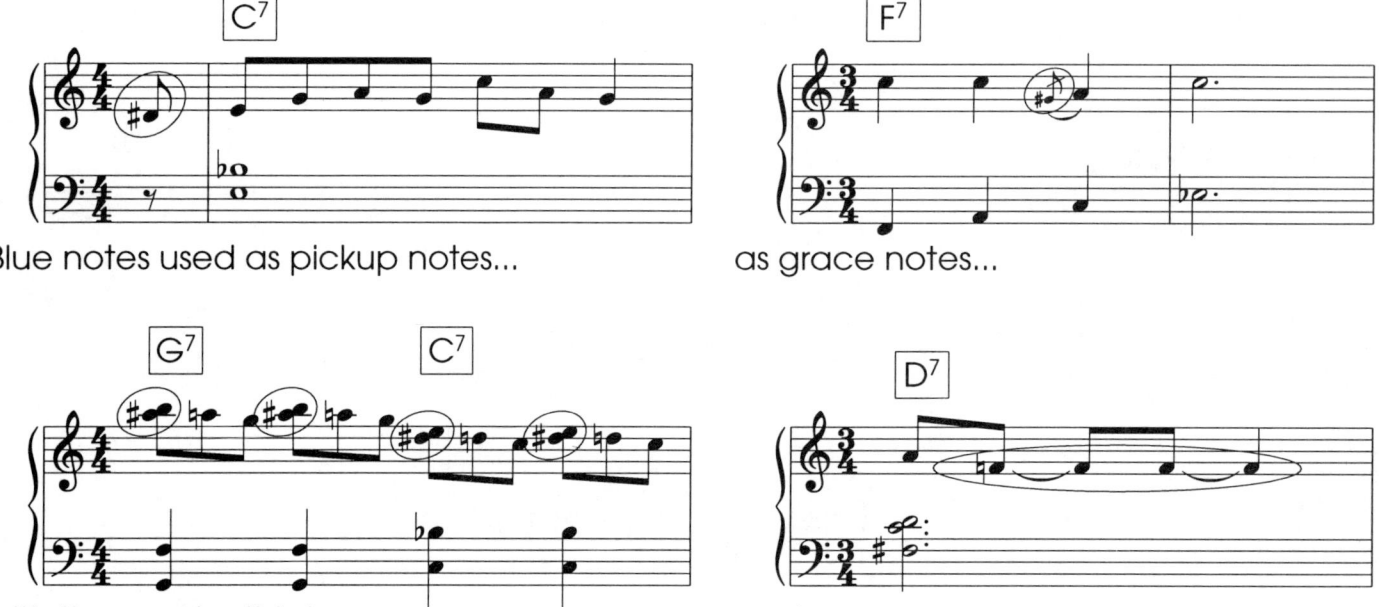

Blue notes used as pickup notes...   as grace notes...

with the regular third...   or alone...

Notice how a blue third and sevenths are used in this line of *HIGHWAY 1*:

When improvising a song in "blues" style, there are now a total of five notes your R.H. can use for each chord. They are the root, third, fifth, seventh, and blue third:

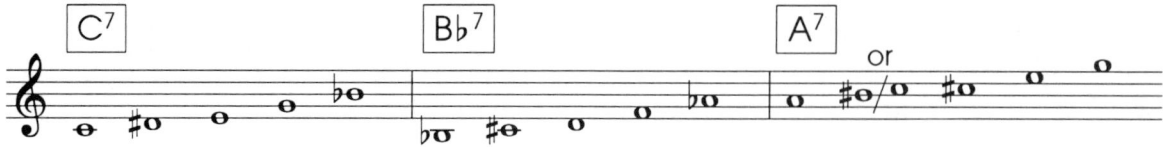

CREATING "LIGHT BLUE"

Improvise, then write in a melody over this "twelve bar" using the five special chord notes. These are root, third, fifth, seventh, and blue note. You could use one of your riffs on pg. 20 with a blue note added, or just go for a whole new thing! ("Swing" is explained on pg. 66.)

LIGHT BLUE

how to b played: _____   written by: _____

Try your song over another LH pattern from pp. 54 & 55!

NINTH CHORDS

You already added sevenths to your chords to add color, or function. You now get to add another piece to the snowman for a total of 5 notes. This is the NINTH CHORD.

When this new note is added to the snowman, it creates the interval of a ninth above the root.

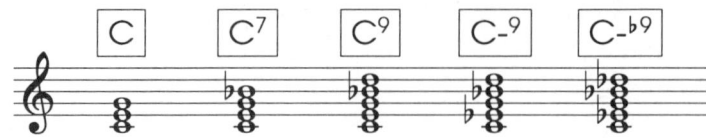

You might also think of it as one whole step higher than the name of the chord. Can you find the 9th in these chords?

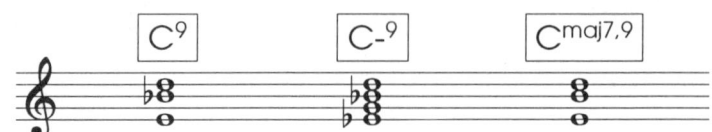

Here are some examples of ninth chords and voicings from songs in this book:

* May be called "A-^{add9}" when seventh should not be added.

24

THIRTEENTH CHORDS

If we continue to build the chord snowman above the ninth, then we add the eleventh and thirteenth. Even though a chord is labelled a 13th, it may still carry the seventh, ninth and eleventh with it. Below is an example of how a C13 chord is formed. (The note which is the 13th of the chord is the same note that is often called the 6th of a chord. Can you tell why?)

C13 CHORD

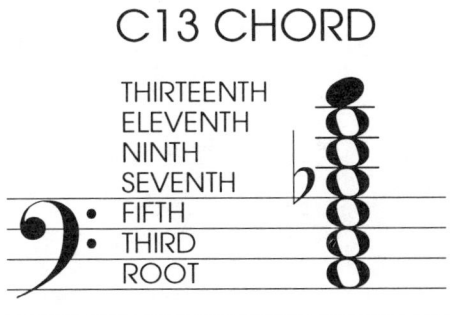

C13 COMMON VOICING

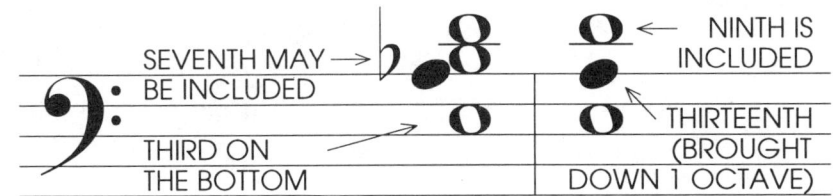

There are too many notes in these chords for your LH to play all at once. When designing your own 13th chord voicings, consider the following:

1. The third and seventh may be the most important notes to include. The function of the chord is described by these notes. Next you may choose from among the fifth, ninth, eleventh and thirteenth. There are many possibilities.

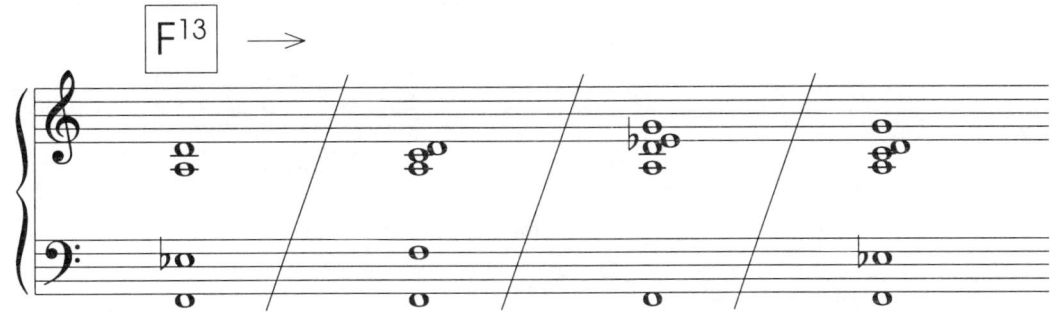

25

2. The notes in the chord just before or just after your 13th chord help determine which voicing to use. Try to use notes that fit the character of the voicings nearby. Perhaps a pattern has been set to follow. Or, perhaps some notes can move by half step or by step to the notes in the other chord.

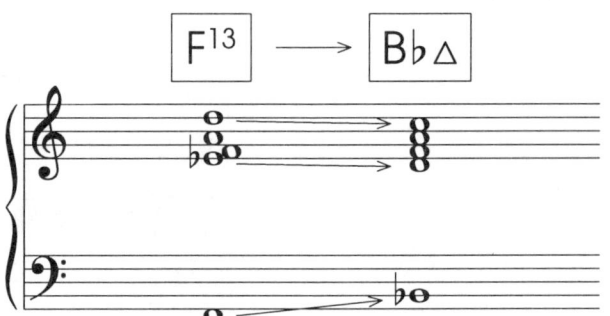

Some notes progressing in opposite directions (contrary motion) create a pleasant transition.

3. A thirteenth chord using only a few notes in its voicing may sound ambiguous. A bass note or additional notes may be needed to help describe the chord. These notes can be in the melody, or added down below, as shown below. Notice in these examples that the three notes of the Dm13 are the same three notes as in the G13. The bass note clears up this problem!

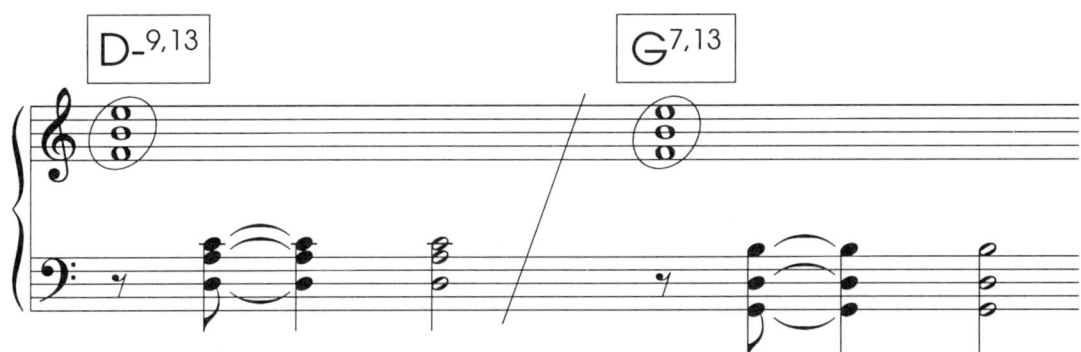

When playing with a group, the bass player may supply the root of the chord

More about chord voicings coming up in Chapter 3!

DIMINISHED & AUGMENTED CHORDS

There are two other qualities that chords can have. Each is used to introduce and strengthen the chord which follows it. Below see how the DIMINISHED CHORD is made. On the next page AUGMENTED CHORDS are explained, and how to use these chromatic chords.

In the DIMINISHED CHORD you will find a snowman with a minor 3rd, (like a minor chord), and lowered 5th.

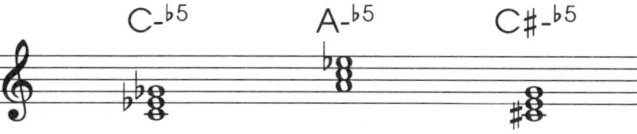

If it has a regular seventh, (like a dominant 7th), then it is called a HALF DIMINISHED SEVENTH.

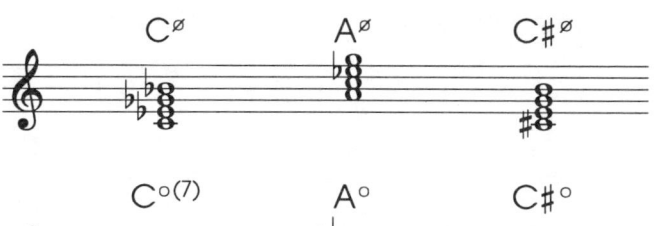

If the seventh is also lowered (or diminished), then it is called a FULLY DIMINISHED SEVENTH CHORD.

Fully diminished chords are quite common. Though they go by many names, they all fit into three categories. The one with the note "C" in it, the one with the note "C#" in it, and the one with "D" in it.

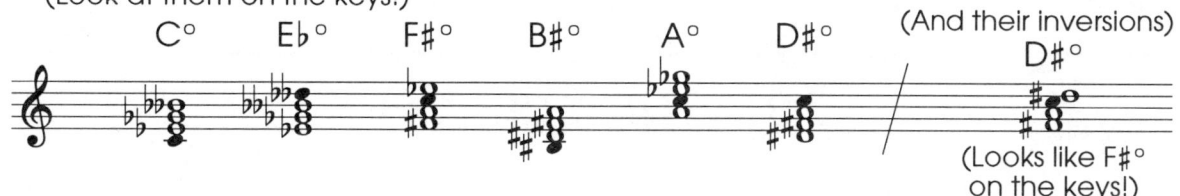

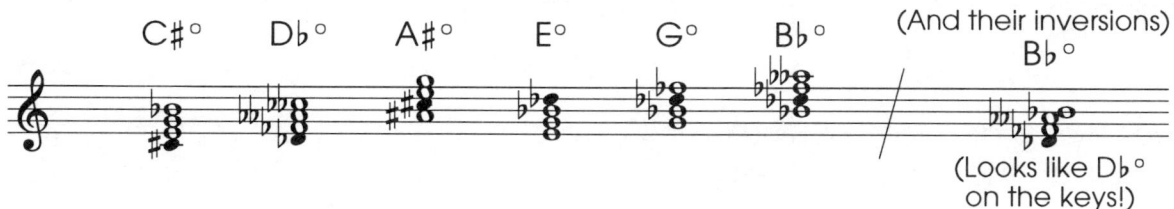

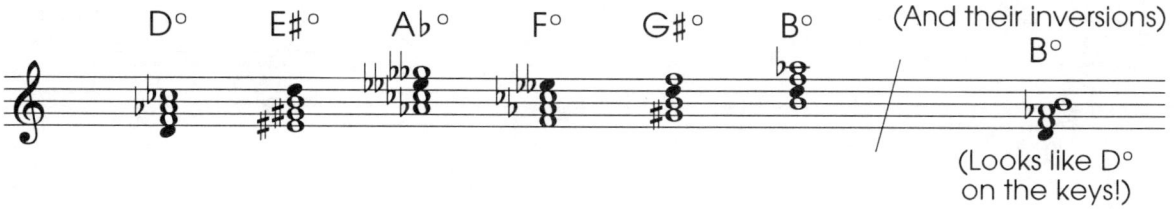

27

To tell which diminished chord to use in your improvisation or composition, you must first establish which chord you are *going to*. You then work backwards to find the right diminished chord.

Choose one of the notes in the chord that you are *going to*. Play the note one half step above or below that note. Create a diminished chord based on that note. (Remember that all notes in a fully diminished chord are always three half steps apart.)

There will be more than one choice. How will you know which one works best?

1. There should be as many half step motions as possible between the note of the diminished chord and the chord which follows. Two works well, three if you can. Better yet, does one half step motion move up to a note, and another one down? Excellent.

2. You like the way it sounds.

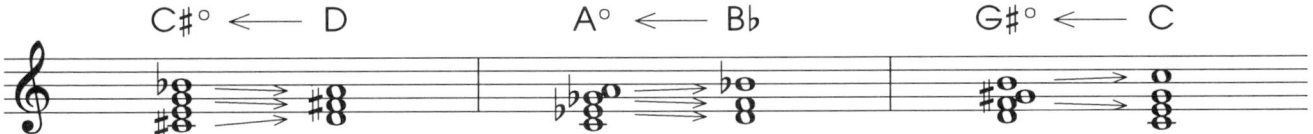

Find a diminished chord to precede each of the following:

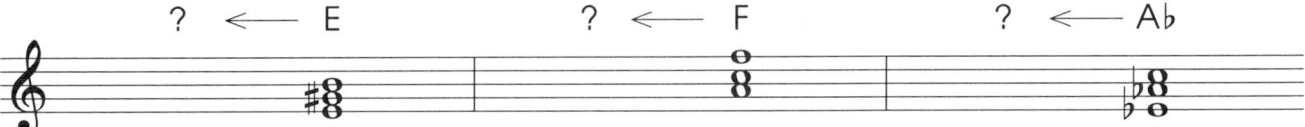

AUGMENTED CHORDS

Augmented chords in their "snowman" shape are like a major chord with the 5th raised a half step.

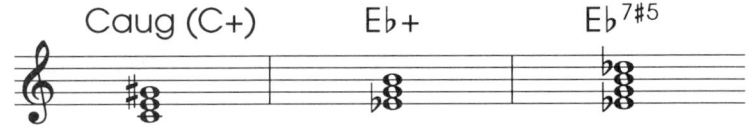

Augmented chords are also a CHROMATIC type chord. They are formed by creating at least one half step motion to the next chord. The augmented chord usually leads to the chord a fourth higher.

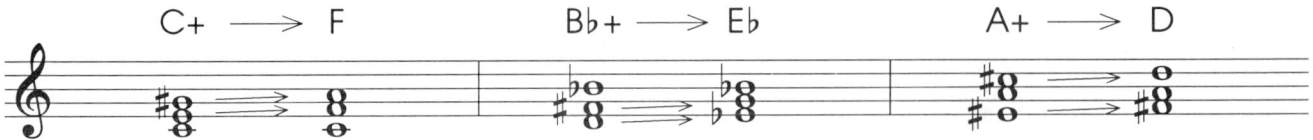

MAJOR/MINOR CHORD SYMBOLS

There are a variety of symbols that identify the quality of a chord. The following chart will assist you as you fake the songs coming up in Chapter 3 and in the FAKEBOOK.

MAJOR CHORDS

These chords are major because they *do not say minor* next to the letter name. Chords are always assumed major unless otherwise stated. So, the word or symbol for *major* next to the letter name applies to the *seventh. These chords all have major sevenths.*

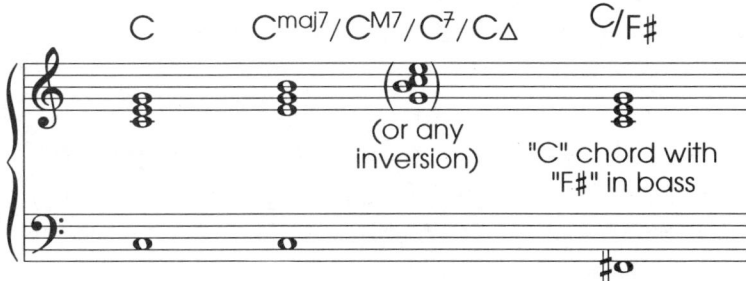

Chords can keep their major 7th quality and still be extended. The plus sign: "+" implies the extension following is sharped. A flat sign: "♭" implies the extension following is flatted. The number "6" means to add only the 13th (same as 6th).

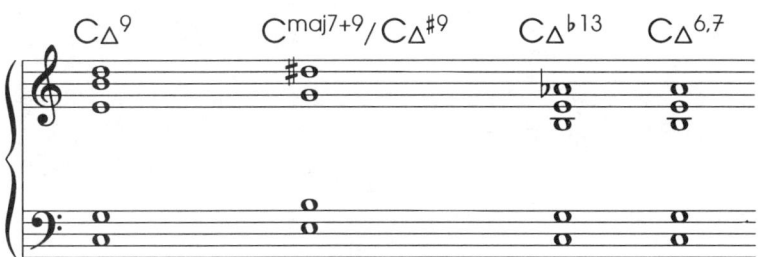

DOMINANT SEVENTH CHORDS

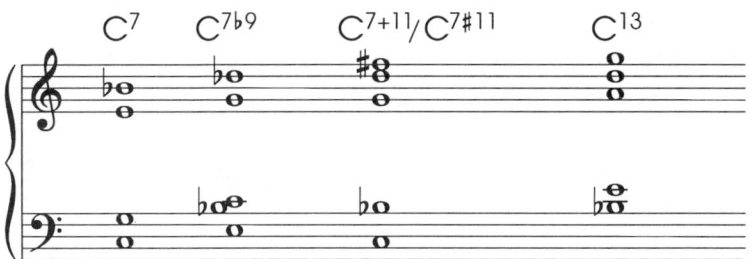

These chords are major chords but have a minor seventh. A minor seventh extension is always implied minor unless stated major as above.

MINOR CHORDS

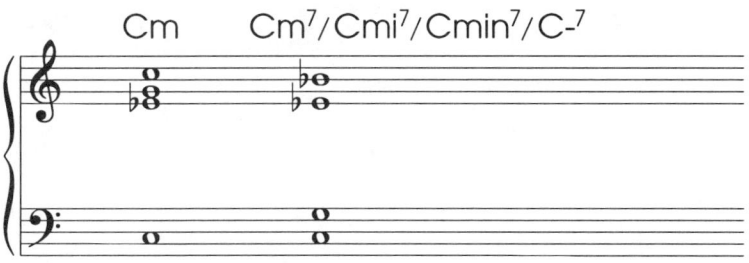

These chords are all minor. The word or symbol for minor relates to the chord and not the seventh.

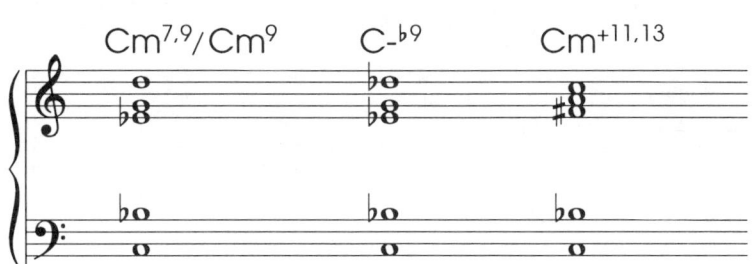

CHAPTER 3   OTHER VOICINGS

CHORD VOICING refers to the arrangement of notes within a chord. Which notes you choose to include, and the arrangement of those notes.

Most jazz artists have their own favorite voicings. Sometimes it is the signature of their style. The types of voicings are unlimited. Here you will find a style that will be useful when COMPING (chording while others play along, or with a soloist). The same info will be handy when accompanying your own RH melody, faking, or in composition.

CHORDS IN FOURTHS

Here's a fun and convenient way of finding jazzy chords that works for comping, CHIPPING (throwing in a little accented beat now and then), or generally pleasant sounds when improvising or faking. *When playing solo, play the root down in the bass just before or after the chord for proof.

FOR MAJOR CHORDS, WITHOUT DOMINANT 7THS

This chord is built from the top down. Your RH will lead the way by choosing a chord and putting its pinky on its name. The next note down will be an interval of a PERFECT FOURTH. This would be exactly 5 half steps down. The next note for the RH will be another perfect fourth. The next two notes are, you guessed it, down two more perfect fourths and played with the LH as shown.

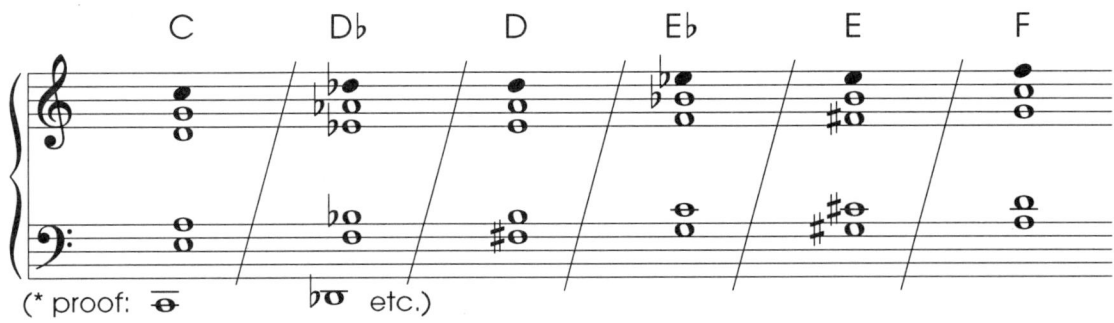

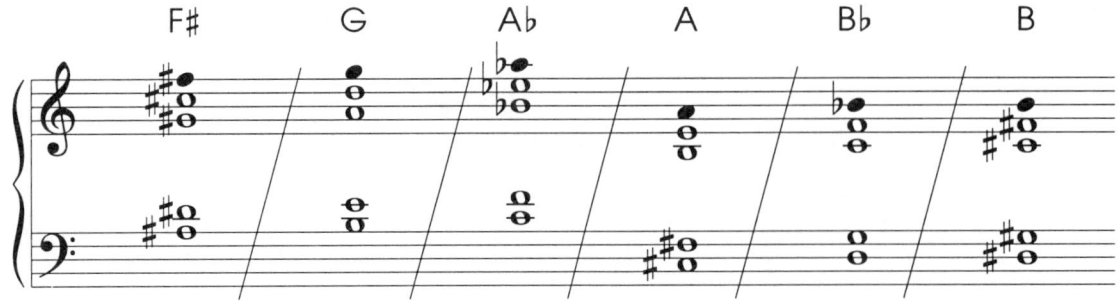

CHECK THIS OUT:

There are two ways to play each chord. It turns out that if you put your RH pinky on the fifth of the chord, building down the exact same way, you have an alternate way of playing the same chord.

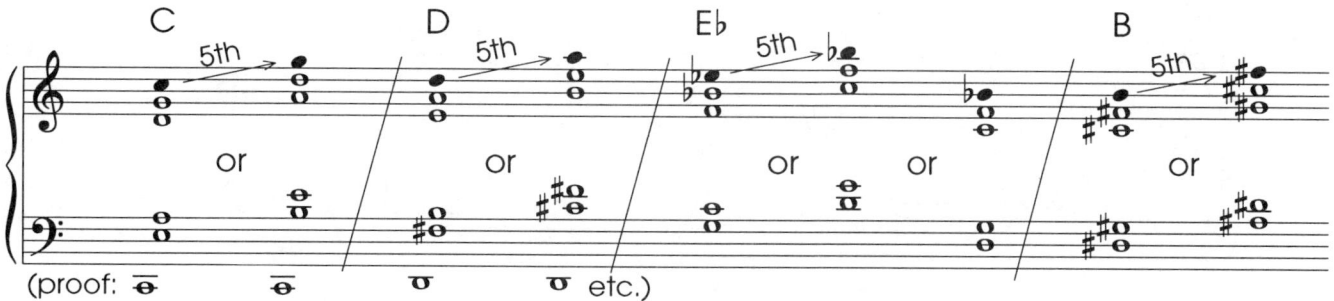

FOR DOMINANT SEVENTH CHORDS

This chord is built from the top down just like the previous chord, but...

If your pinky starts on the chord name then the fourth note down must be brought <u>up a half step</u>. That note which was the 13th of the chord has now become the 7th of the chord.

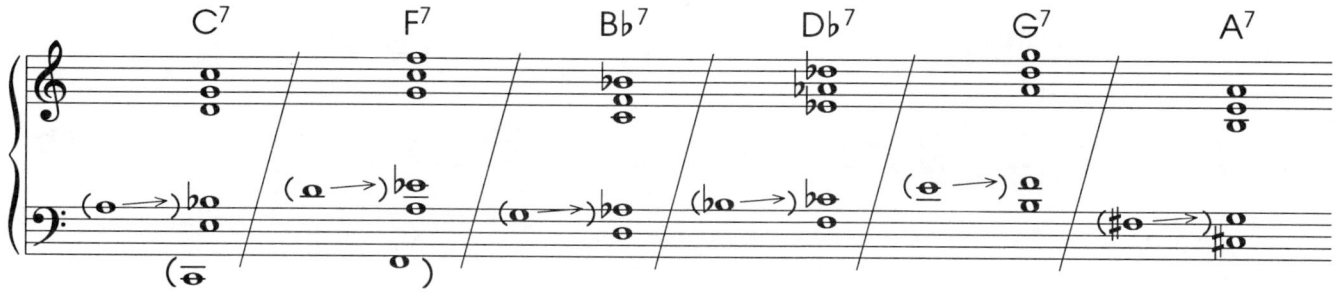

If your pinky starts on the fifth of the chord, then the bottom-most note must be <u>lowered a half step</u> to create a seventh.

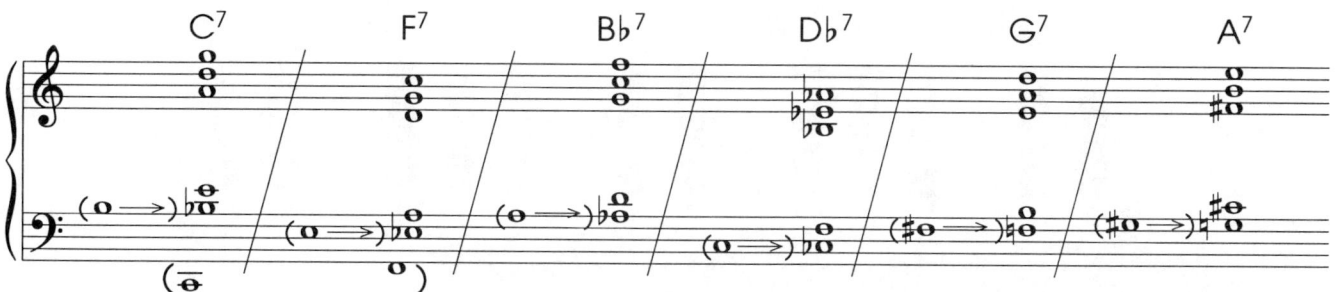

FOR MINOR CHORDS

To form a minor chord in fourths, simply put your RH pinky on the minor third of the chord. Build the fourths down as usual. These chords will automatically have the seventh built in.

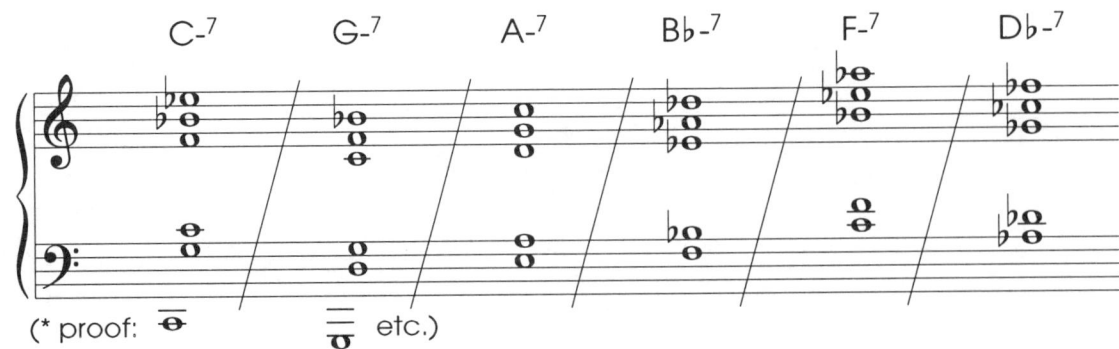

Notice that the five notes of the following chord can have three names. In order to explain to the listener which chord they are hearing, you might add a bass note before or after playing it. Sometimes the chord is clear without doing this. Perhaps there is repetition, or you have a bass player playing along, or the melody notes clarified the chord.

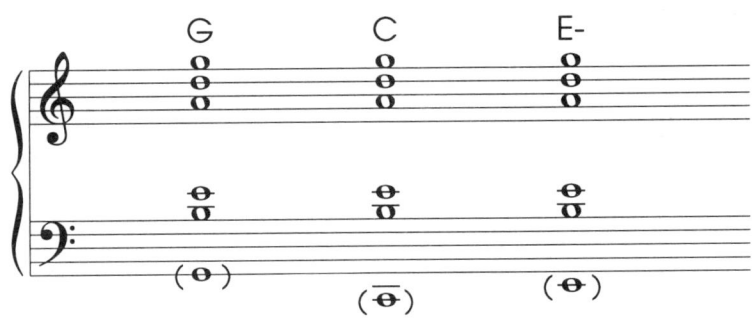

A word about range...

All of these chords in fourths seem to sound best when the RH pinky starts within the range shown below. A bit higher or lower may sound OK in some situations.

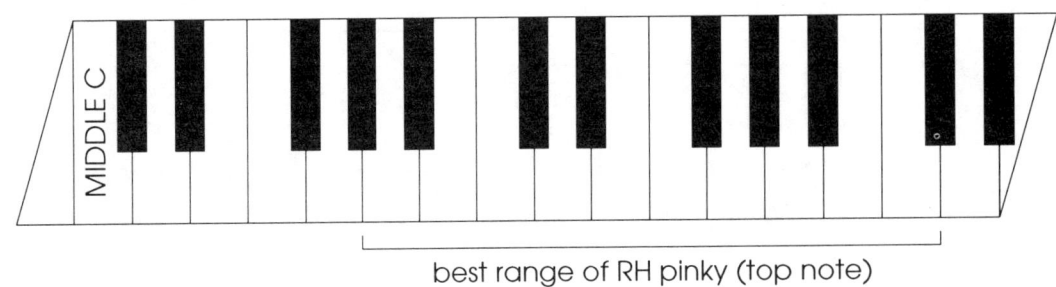

APPLE BETTY ANYONE?

Here's a chance to practice your chords in fourths with a LEAD LINE (just melody and chord symbols given). Below are the first eight measures of "Apple Betty" written out for you in a jazz waltz style using chords in fourths. Finish the song by improvising or writing in the same style.

Each note of this melody serves as the top note of a chord in fourths.

In the chords required, flat the ninth by lowering the second RH note down. (These chords have the 5th on top.)

APPLE BETTY

Jazz Waltz, Swing (pg. 66)

U.A.R.

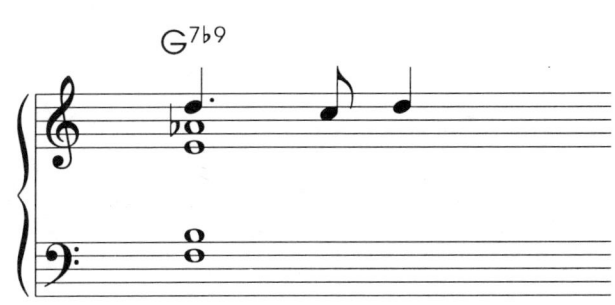

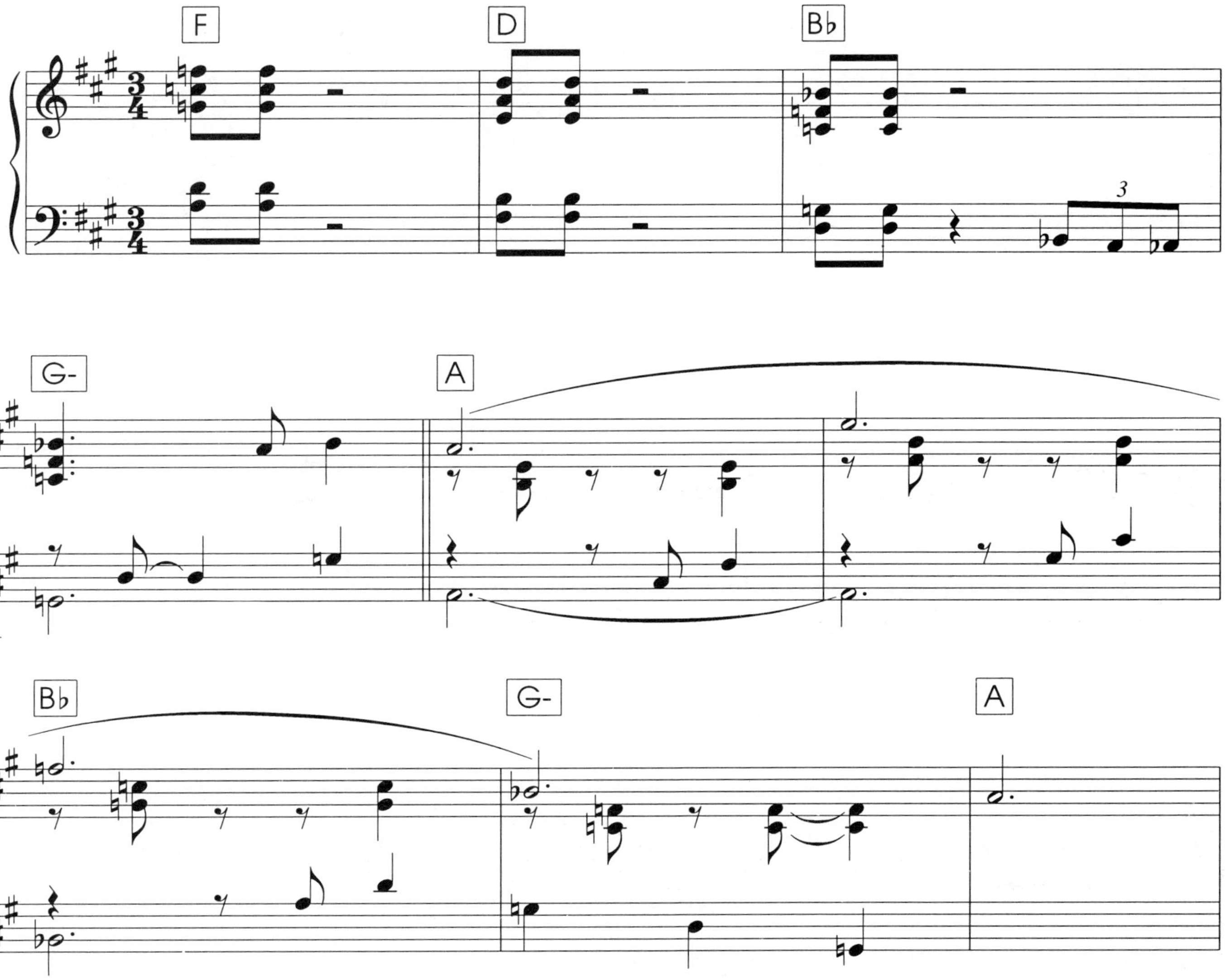

© 1998 BY MEL BAY PUBLICATIONS, INC., PACIFIC, MO 63069.
ALL RIGHTS RESERVED. INTERNATIONAL COPYRIGHT SECURED. B.M.I.

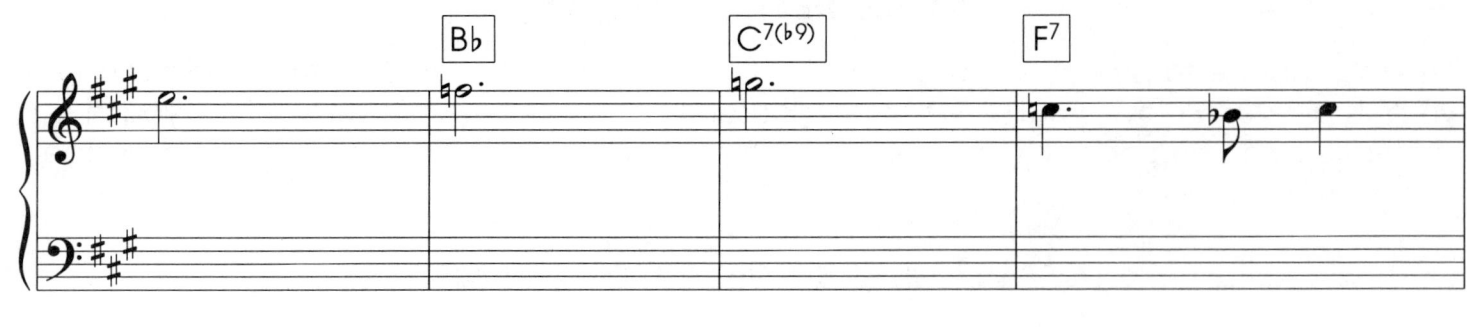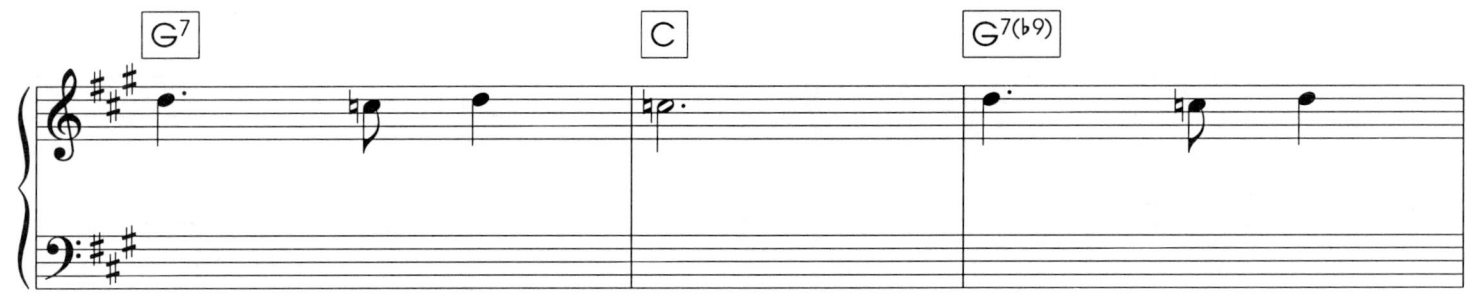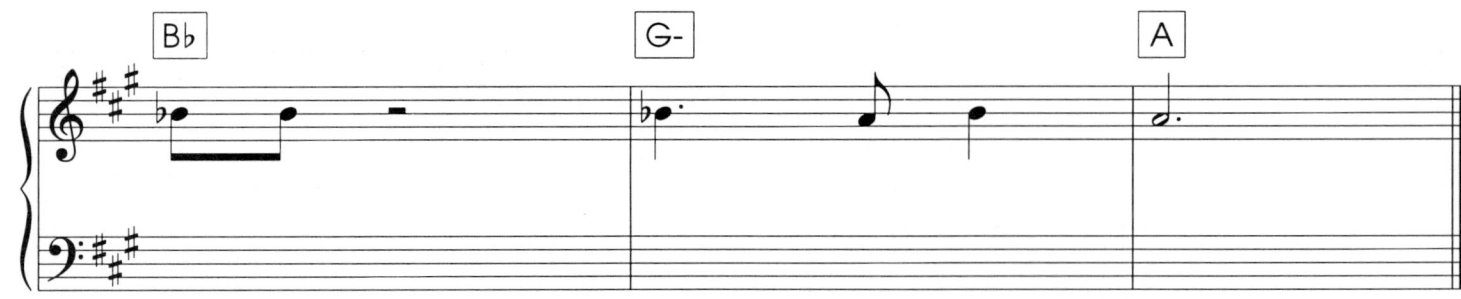

LEFT HAND VOICINGS (IN FOURTHS)

A convenient LH voicing that has a similar quality to the ones on the previous pages is actually quite simple to do. Play the lower three notes of the chords in fourths to leave your RH free to make a melody or improvise. These voicings sound best when the top note is near or above middle C, so a melody may need to be played an octave higher than written.

For example:

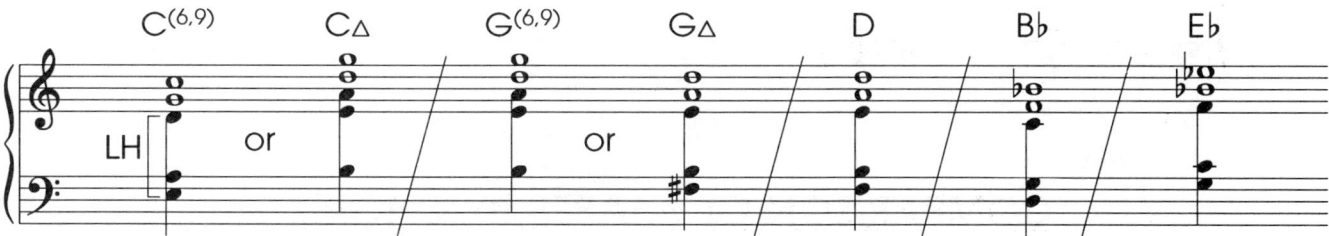

For major chords:
1. LH thumb begins one step above the root, or one step above the fifth.
2. Then build the next two fourths down.

These voicings in fourths below have an added note in the middle for a fuller sound. In general, you may add the note a whole step below the middle note.

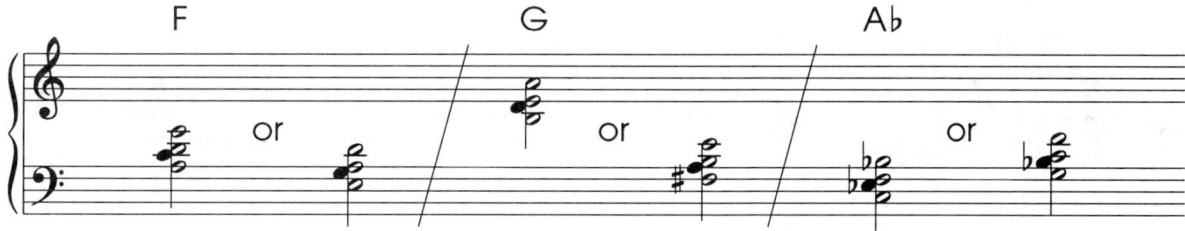

To add a seventh:
  If you begin one step higher than the root, add the note a half step above the middle note. (You may keep the middle note, though.)

If you begin one step higher than the fifth, lower the bottom a half step.

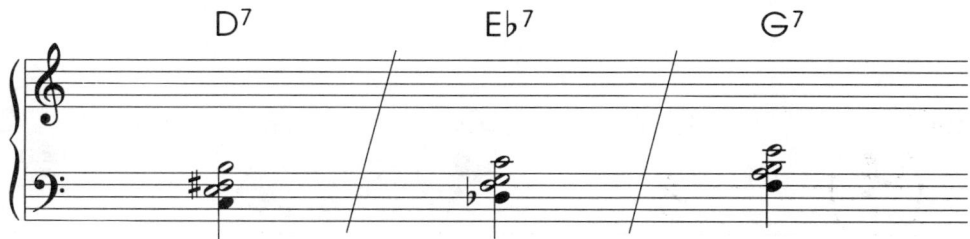

For minor chords:
To create this LH alone chord in fourths, use the same shape as the major chord that begins one note higher than the root. Lower the bottom a half step. (You may notice that this same shape could be called a different chord if a different bass note was given below it!)

COMPARISON OF SHAPES BY CHORD
(*for LH alone chords in fourths)

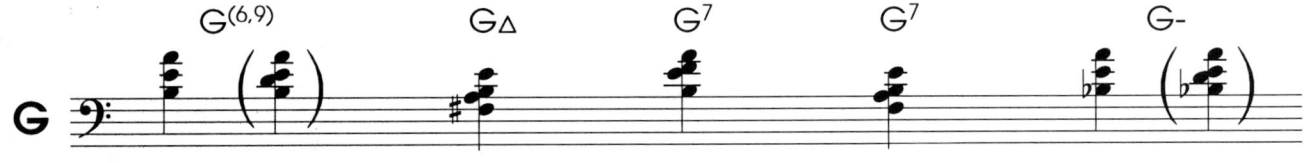

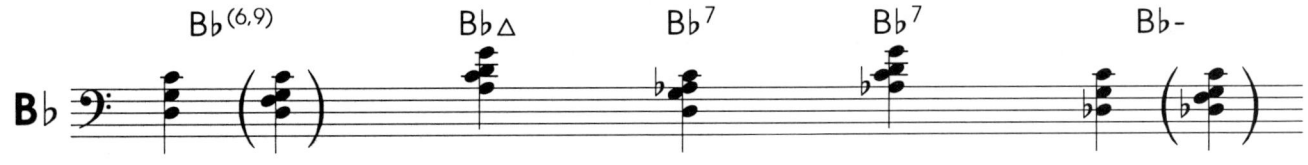

* Generally, begin with your LH thumb at or above middle C for these shapes.

Easier voicings may serve a song well. Or perhaps there is a chord quality that's called for and you haven't time to design something! A root chord, or partial chord may do just fine. If you select just two notes to play rather than the thicker quality of the chords in fourths, then choose the third and seventh.

Play these chords from the twelve bar "HIGHWAY 1". Notice how the third and seventh from each chord sound good and create good voice leading.

In the song "FLAP JACKS" some chords use the third and seventh. The voice leading between the first two chords, for instance, smoothly moves into the root and third. Can you find and circle all the chords using thirds <u>and</u> sevenths?

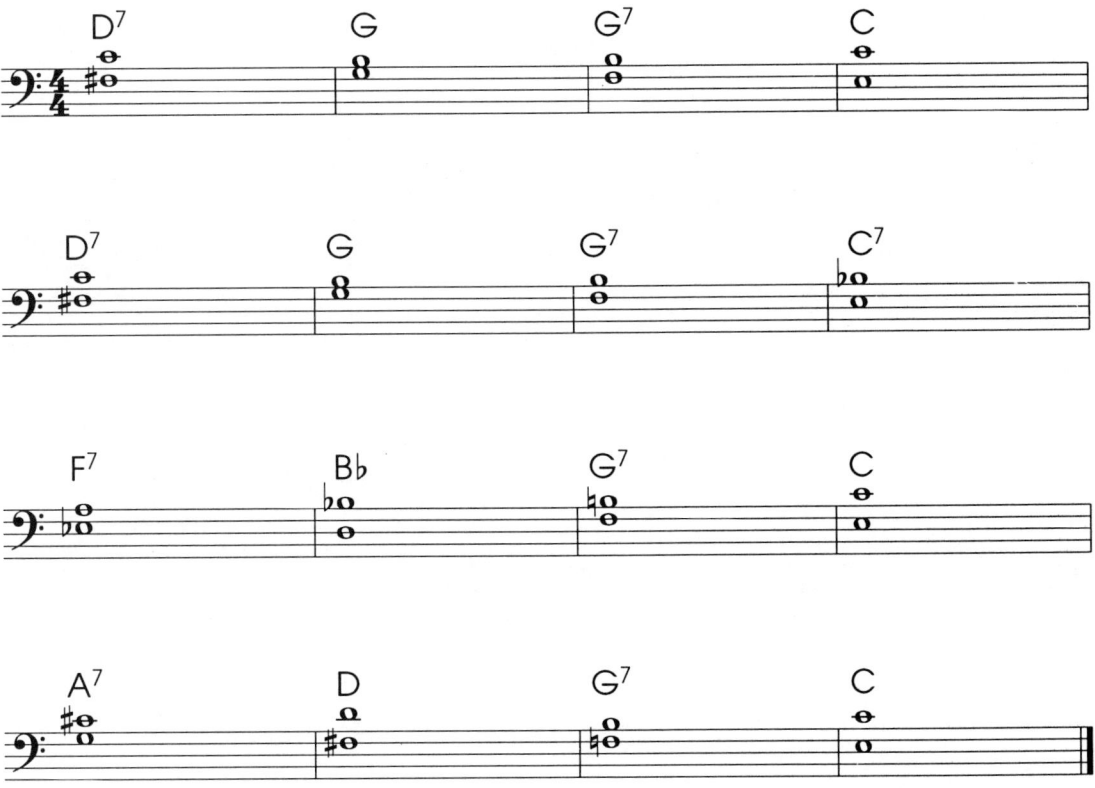

Playing LH chords in fourths offers choices for each chord. In the following song, FAR AWAY PLACES, some LH chord suggestions are given at the beginning. Experiment with some shapes as you continue faking through the rest of the song.

FAR AWAY PLACES

U.A.R

Can you identify the chords in the following cuts from songs in this book?

THE HESITATING BLUES:

FIESTA:

THE HAPPY DEE HOMEMAKER SHOW:

CHAPTER 4 — MODES AND SUCH

Lets say there's a long note in the melody. You would like to make those few beats or measures more fancy. You could do some rhythm things with the chord, or bring out the LH accompaniment part. But what if you could show off your musical dexterity, and good musical taste, by running up and down the keys with some scale-like patterns?

MODES are like variations of scales. The Ionian mode is the same as a major scale. Begin on the second note of that scale and you create a Dorian mode. You can begin on the third note to create Phrygian, and so on as shown below. All seven modes in the following example are shown from the perspective of a C scale and have the same notes in them. However, because their starting notes are different, they will have different functions.

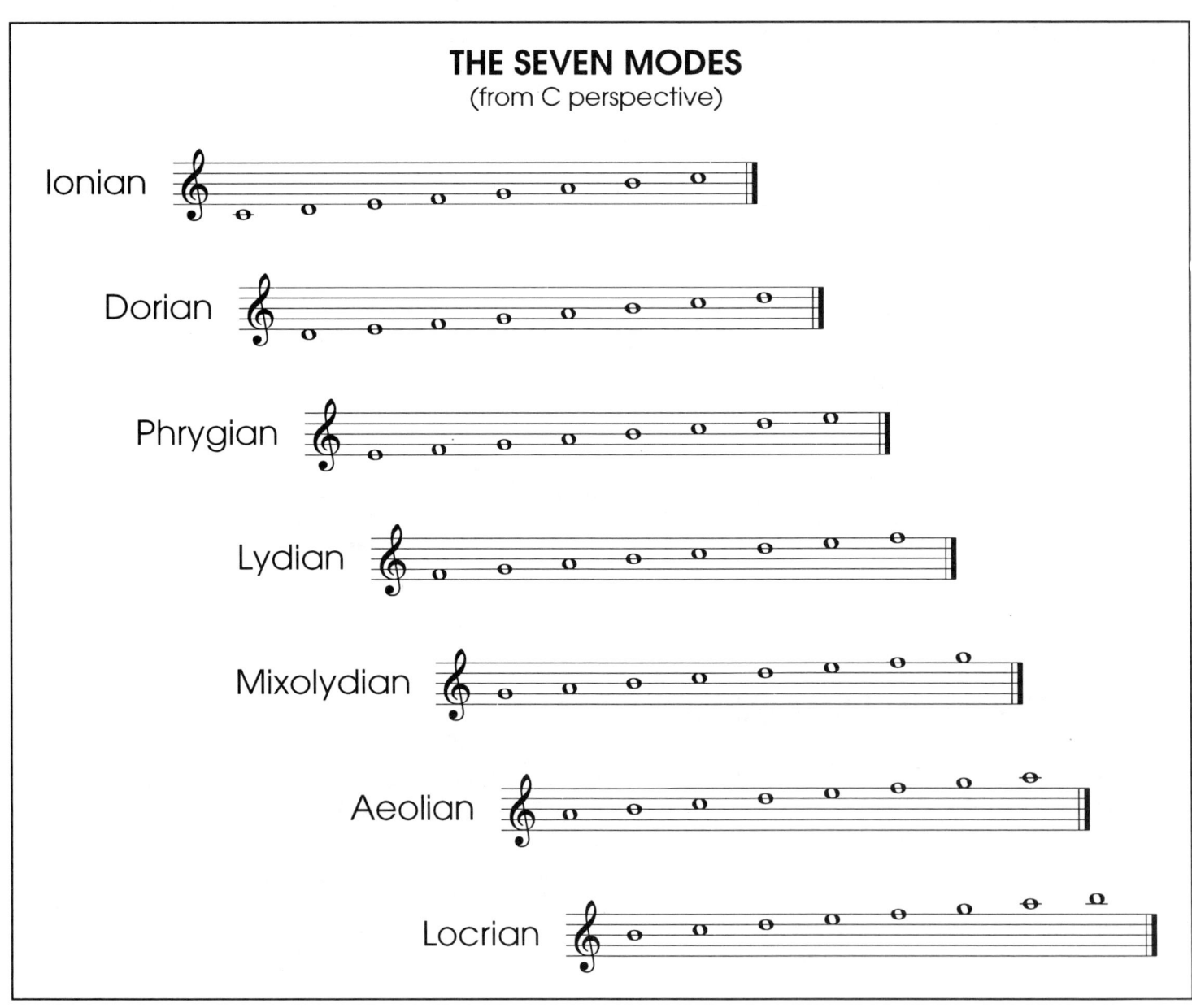

A mode's name tells which note of the original scale it begins on. For instance:

IONIAN means you are starting on the same note as the original scale.

DORIAN means that this mode's first note will begin
on the 2nd step of the original scale.

MIXOLYDIAN (or MIXO) means that this mode's first note will begin
on the 5th step of the original scale.

B♭ perspective:
(B♭ scale)

DORIAN on C:
Notes from the B♭ scale, but starting on C.
(Think: I'm starting on the 2nd step
of the B♭ scale.)

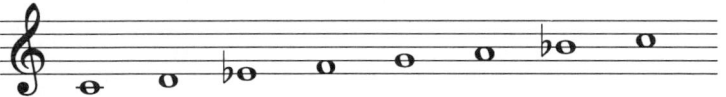

MIXO(LYDIAN) on F:
Notes from the B♭ scale, but starting on F.
(Think: I'm starting on the 5th step
of the B♭ scale.)

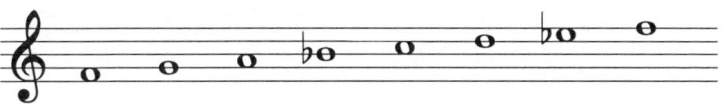

YES! THERE'S ANOTHER WAY TO FIND A MODE!

Here's another way of finding the three modes: IONIAN, DORIAN, & MIXO. These are the three modes you'll use the most.

Note the difference between *Ionian on C* (regular C scale) and *Dorian on C*.

C D E F G A B C | C D (E♭) F G A (B♭) C

Dorian has 3rd and 7th lowered!

Note the difference between *Ionian on C* (regular C scale) and *Mixo on C*.

C D E F G A B C | C D E F G A (B♭) C

Mixo has 7th lowered!

If you think of them the way shown in the boxes, you won't need to refer back to another key signature. Instead, just make the adjustment needed to fit a given chord. You'll need to know your key signatures very well! See pg. 10.

MATCHING MODES

Notes from a mode are used in a melodic way, and usually with the RH. They may help create a melody, be decoration added to existing melody notes; or be used to create a melody like improvisation. But first you have to know which one to use! Below are three of the modes from the examples on page 40. These are the ones used the most.

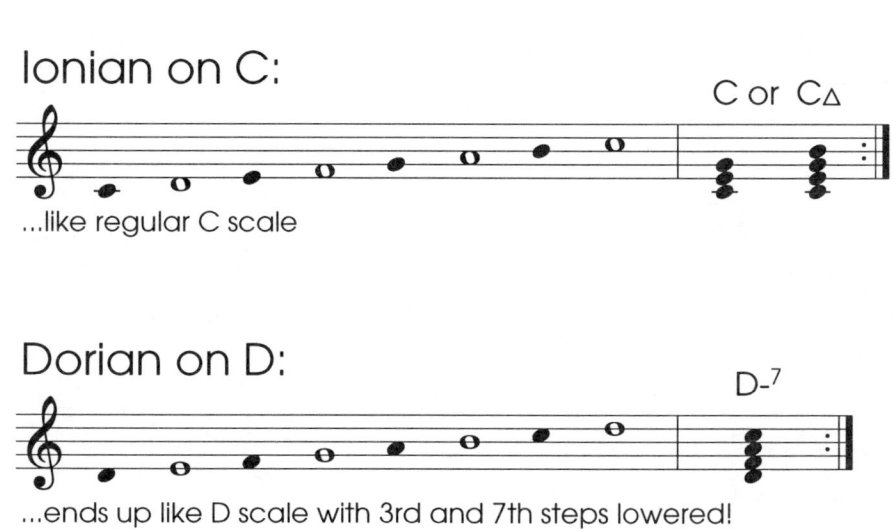

Take the first note of each mode, then add every other note to create a three or four note snowman.

Notice that the resulting chords have different qualities. One is a MAJOR 7th, one a MINOR 7th, and one a DOMINANT 7th.

Now for some generalities about the
PROPERTIES OF THESE THREE MODES

The notes of an <u>IONIAN MODE</u> work well when playing above a <u>MAJOR CHORD</u>.
(This mode is the same as a major scale.)

The notes of a <u>DORIAN MODE</u> work well when playing above a <u>MINOR SEVENTH CHORD</u>.
(This mode is like a major scale with the 3rd and 7th steps lowered.)

The notes of a <u>MIXO MODE</u> will work well when playing above a <u>DOMINANT 7TH CHORD</u>.
(This mode is like a major scale with the 7th step lowered.)

Write and play the following modes and chords, then listen to them played together.

	RH Mode to play above it (insert correct accidentals):	LH Chord:
Ionian on E	E F♯ G♯ A B C♯ D♯ E	E
Ionian on D♭		
Dorian on G		
Dorian on B		
Mixo on D		
Mixo on C		

List the correct (RH) mode needed for the following LH chords:

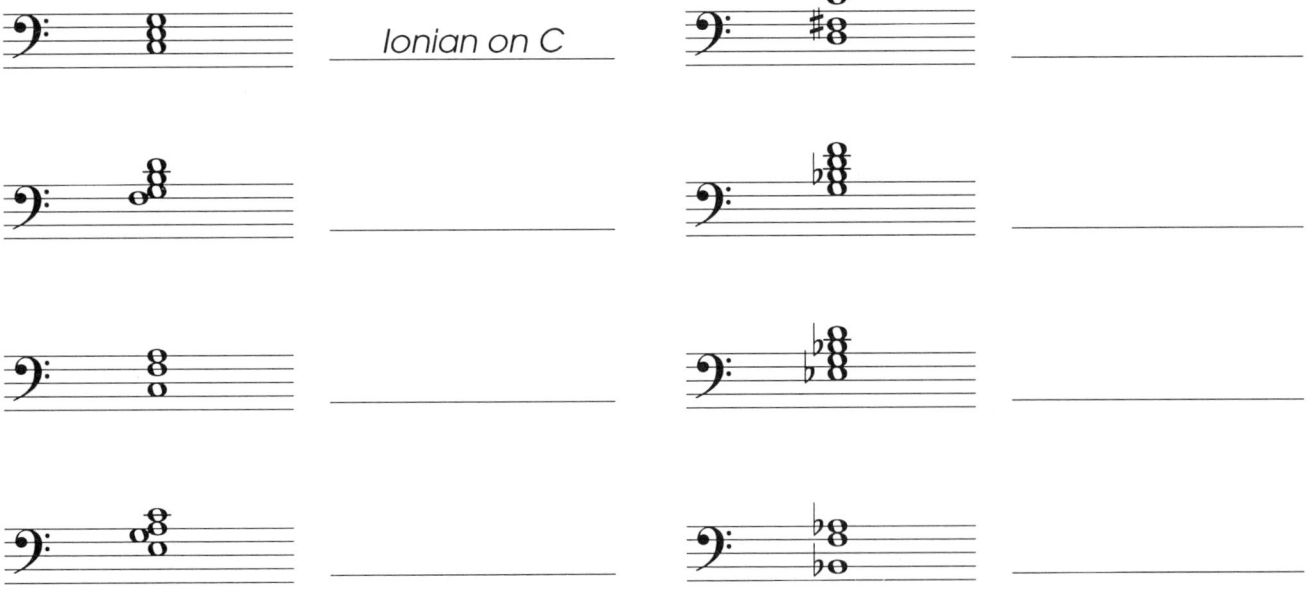

Ionian on C

44

USING MODES

If you were using modal notes to improvise over the chords D-⁷ and G⁷, you would note that the notes for each mode would be the same (see pg. 40). That's because both of those chords fit into the key of C.

Dorian on D (second step of C scale)   Mixo on G (fifth step of C scale)

But jazz songs often use chords that are out of the key. That's when the game of which modal notes to use becomes more interesting. In the following examples, the notes of the melody will be replaced by examples of modal improv. First the modes are figured out, and then different patterns are suggested to use with them.

...original melody:

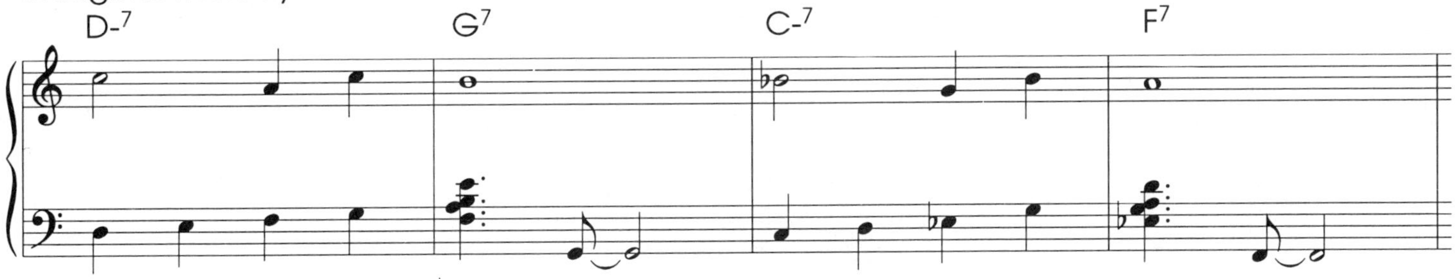

D-⁷   G⁷   C-⁷   F⁷

D-⁷ Dorian on D

G⁷ Mixo on G

C-⁷ Dorian on C

F⁷ Mixo on F

...possible modal improv:

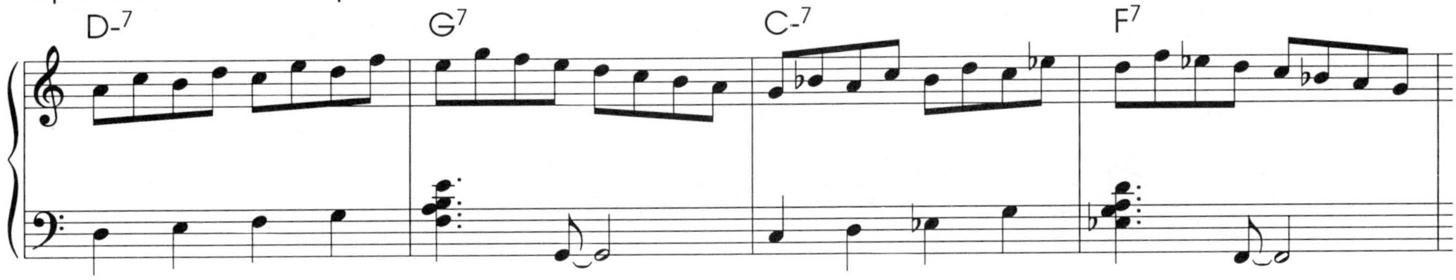

D-⁷   G⁷   C-⁷   F⁷

For practice, play through the song "Oh When The Saints Go Marchin' In." During the long notes you can decorate with some modal fill. Keep that LH chord pattern going! (LH accompaniment patterns are on pp. 54 & 55.) Then play once again, this time improvising a modal fill in the RH *instead* of the melody. Below are suggested patterns for your modal fill, but there are lots more on the next page that you can try!

OH, WHEN THE SAINTS GO MARCHIN' IN

traditional

© 1998 BY MEL BAY PUBLICATIONS, INC., PACIFIC, MO 63069.
ALL RIGHTS RESERVED. INTERNATIONAL COPYRIGHT SECURED. B.M.I.

(Notice that only the C⁷ chord will call for a mode with any accidentals. Can you tell why?)

Try one of these examples for your modal fill pattern:

example 1:

example 2:

With the song "Verna" you will have a chance to experiment with a variety of different modes in the same song. First, listen to the melody adding a faked LH. Then mix and match paterns as you play through once again with modal fill. Some chords don't last very long, but you have the option of just using a chord arpeggio in those measures, if you want. Be creative! Be brave!

VERNA

U.A.R

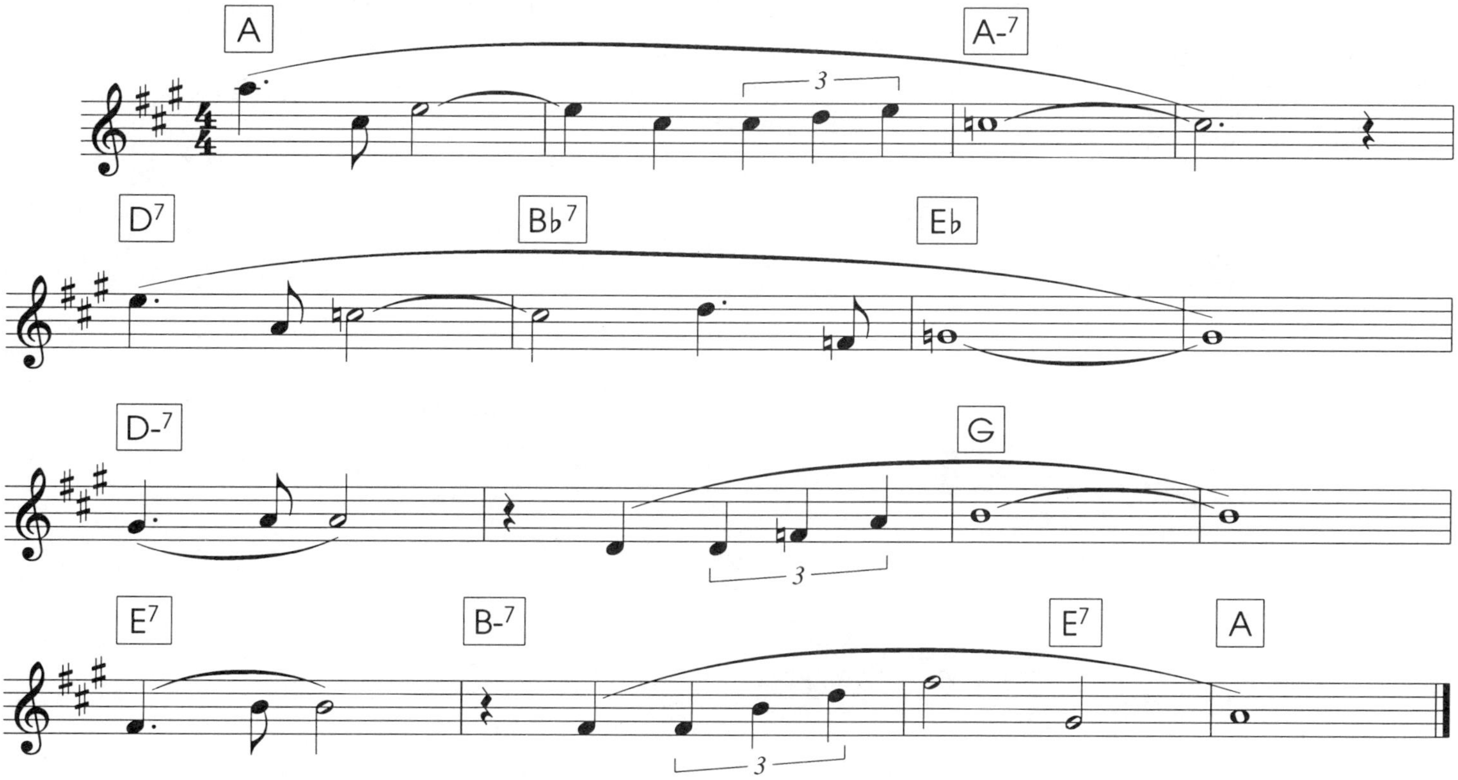

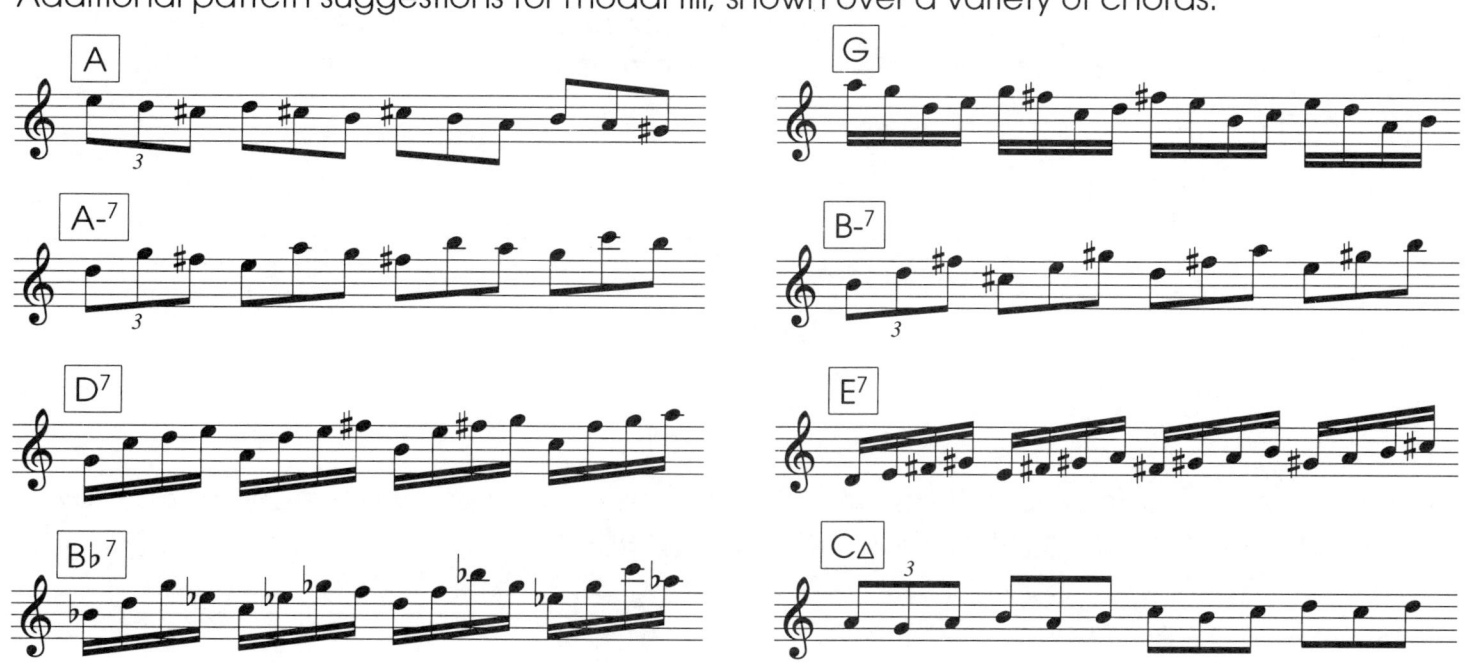

Additional pattern suggestions for modal fill, shown over a variety of chords:

BLUES SCALE

The BLUES SCALE will be very convenient to use when improvising and creating blues and related styles. It's a scale-like arrangement of notes for the melody hand, usually the RH, to play. Its design makes it fun to use because any order of its notes can be played *over* the I, IV, or V chord, as in a twleve bar (pg. 13), and you don't change the scale when the chords do! Just stay in the blues scale of the key you're in.

The C blues scale is formed by taking only notes that are found twice among the I, IV, and V chords for the key of C. This includes the blue third (pg. 22) and seventh for each chord. Blues style songs like to add sevenths to the I, IV and V chords.

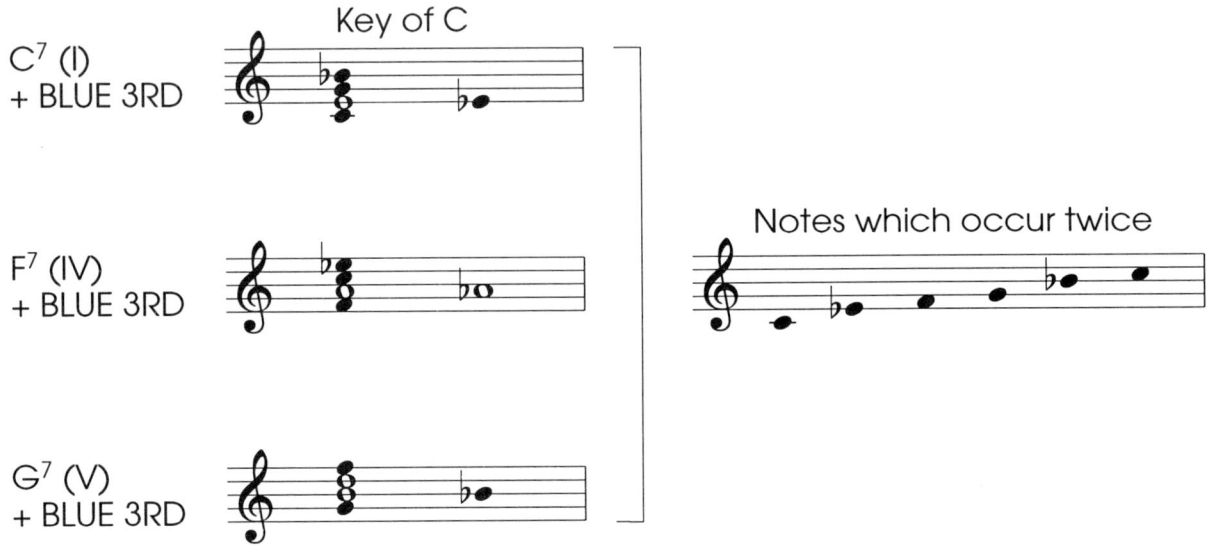

The complete blues scale adds a G♭ (F♯). This connects both halves of the scale and creates two half steps, one between F and G♭ and another between G♭ and G.

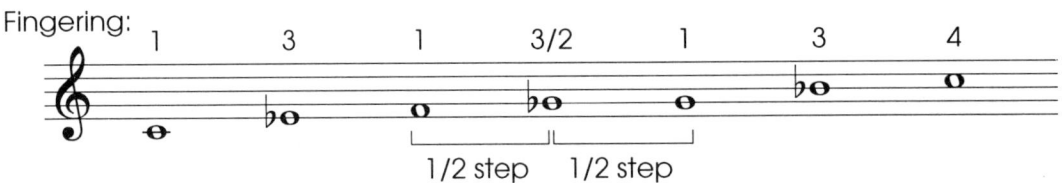

There is more than one proper fingering. Different riffs moving up or down this scale may feel better with another fingering than the one suggested here.

Here are seven common blues keys with corresponding blues scales.

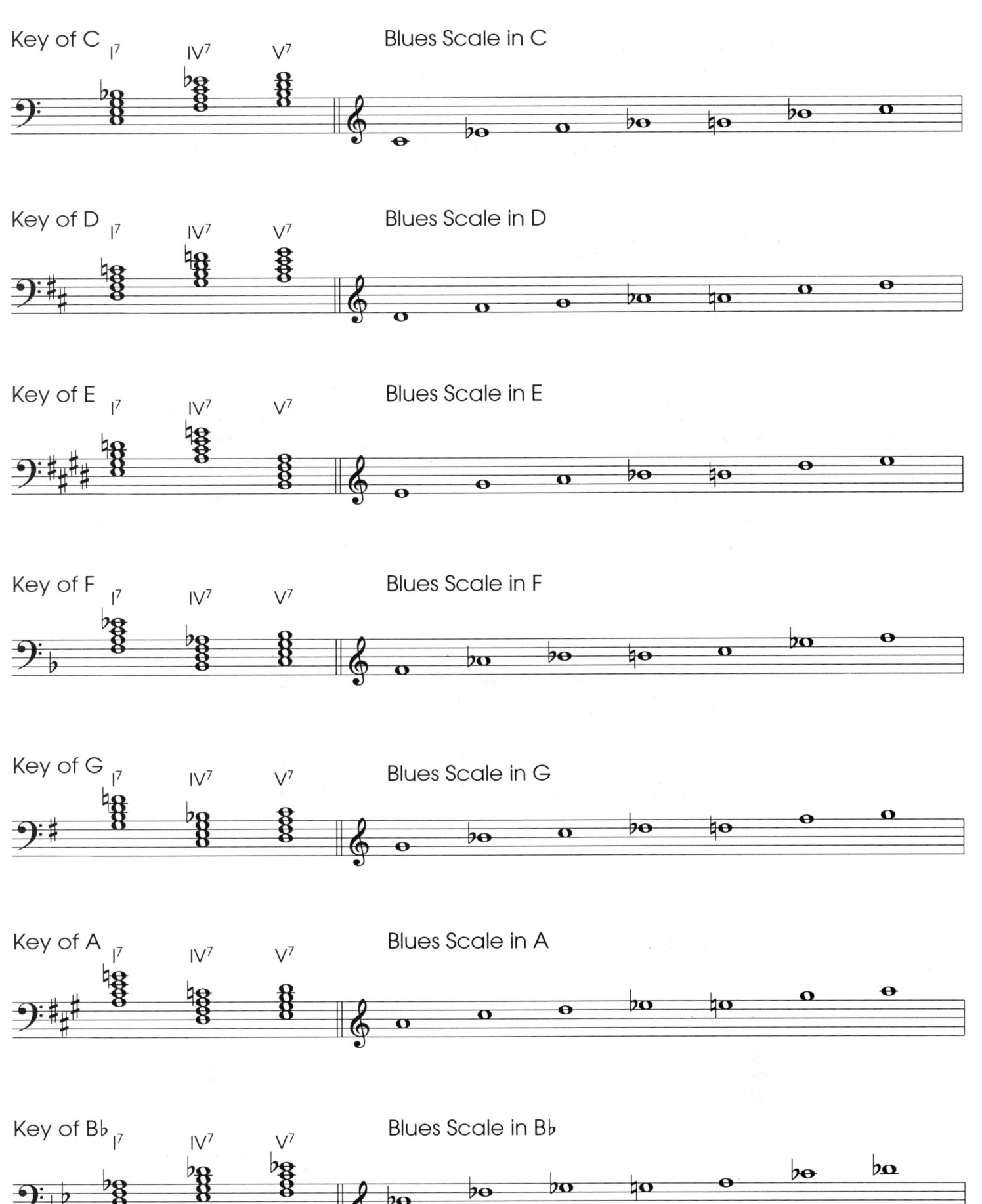

USING THE BLUES SCALE

While the LH chords of a twelve bar change, the RH stays with the notes from the respective blues scale and creates a good sounding improvised line. You do not have to use notes from the chords, just the blues scale.

Listen to this D blues scale riff as it plays over the I, IV, and V chords in the key of D.

Blues riff:

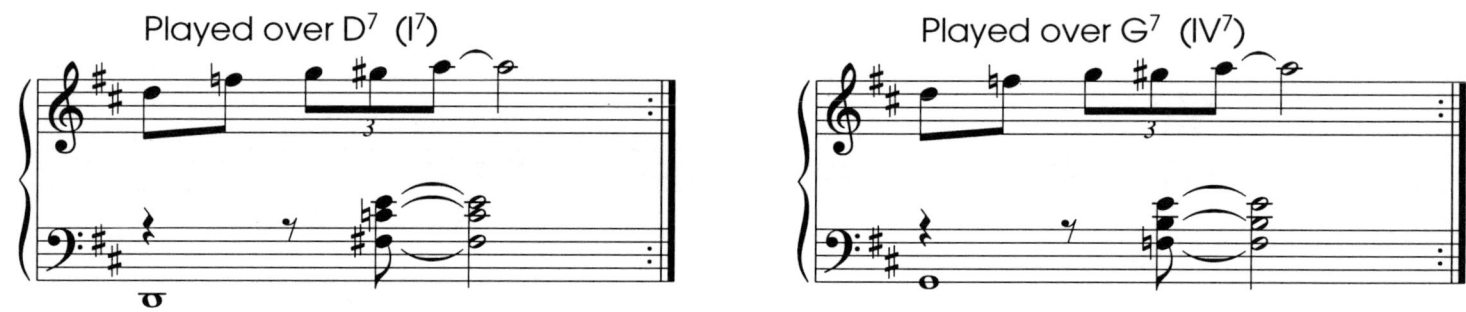

Try your hand at writing a D blues scale riff. Then play it over the I IV and V chords, as above, to hear how it sounds!

Your D blues scale riff:

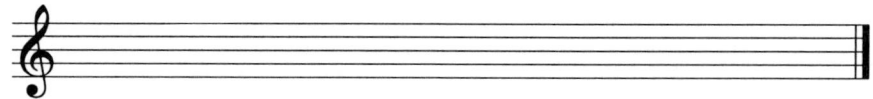

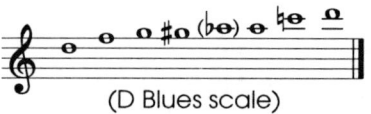
(D Blues scale)

Now try your hand at improvising with the F blues scale over the changes to "Highway 1."*
You'll be surprised how some random choices of notes and patterns using this scale can
create an interesting RH melody or improvised line. Remember, these F blues scale notes
will work over all the chord changes. Start with some long notes and short patterns first,
soon you'll be able to create something faster and fancier!

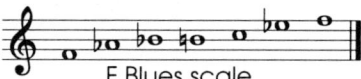
F Blues scale

HIGHWAY 1, DETOUR!

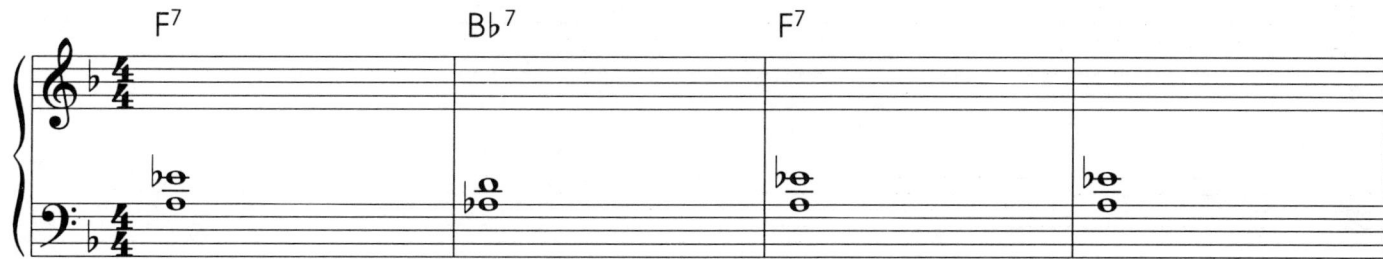

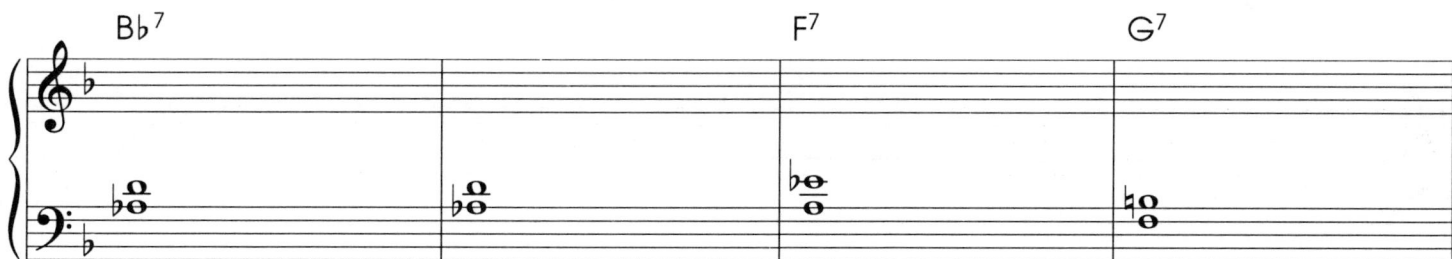

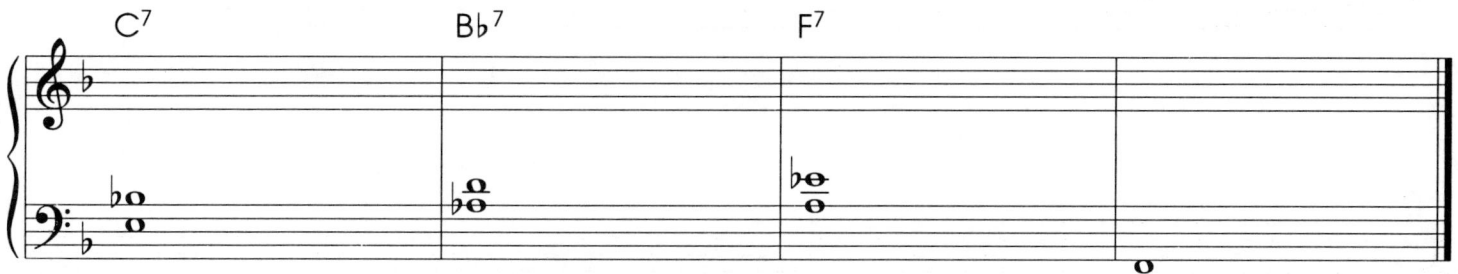

© 1998 BY MEL BAY PUBLICATIONS, INC., PACIFIC, MO 63069.
ALL RIGHTS RESERVED. INTERNATIONAL COPYRIGHT SECURED. B.M.I.

*This twelve bar pattern is a variation of the regular twelve bar pattern (pg. 15). It is:

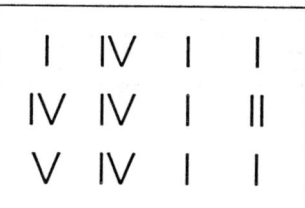

Here are another two variations of the twelve bar pattern to experiment with:

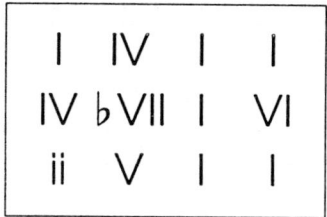 (Last bar can be V if repeating.)

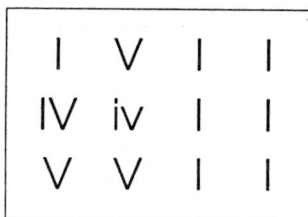 (Last bar can be V if repeating.)

51

FAKEBOOK

When you FAKE a song, you are creating a style and arrangement to the chords of a given melody. You may decide to use a repeating LH pattern, add harmony to the RH, vary the melody a bit, or go off on a RH design fantasy.

The accompaniments are limitless. You might begin by using the LH patterns listed below and on the next page. Simply match an appropriate one, and one you like, to one of the songs prepared for you in the charts of this FAKEBOOK. These accompaniment patterns are suggesitons to get started. You'll discover some of your own, perhaps even creating your own style. To get out of your LH's way, melodies are often played an octave higher.

If you don't already, you'll get to know your chords well as you create complete songs from just a melody line and chord symbols!

ACCOMPANIMENT PATTERNS
(...with spaces at the end to write in some of your own discoveries...)

*Eighth note patterns may swing.

GETTING STARTED

Below each faking chart you'll notice suggested pattern numbers that will work for you. Here are two examples of how this works:

Here's the first line of "JAMBO" as it appears in this FAKEBOOK:

5, 8, 9, 10

Here's how it would sound with suggested pattern #5:

It will sound like this with suggested pattern #10:

> Even the melody line can be personalized! Add notes, harmonize, or change the rhythms if you want. And don't forget that these melodies often work well played an octave higher than written.

ANYWHERE

U.A.R.

APPLE BETTY

U.A.R.

26 (see pg. 35), 31

© 1998 BY MEL BAY PUBLICATIONS, INC., PACIFIC, MO 63069.
ALL RIGHTS RESERVED. INTERNATIONAL COPYRIGHT SECURED. B.M.I.

FIERO

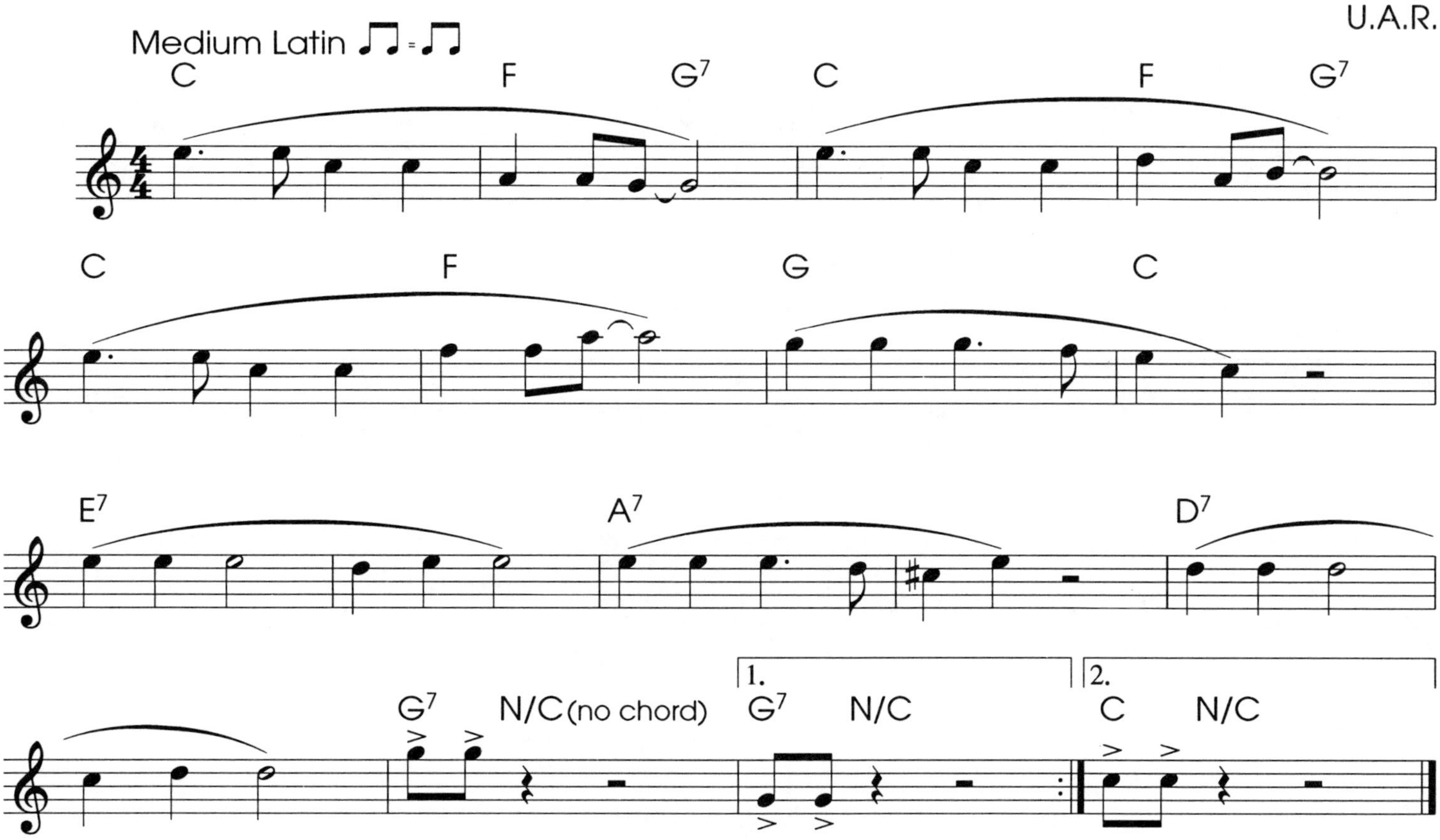

INCH O' BLUES

U.A.R.

6, 11, 18, 24

© 1998 BY Mel Bay PUBLICATIONS, INC., PACIFIC, MO 63069.
ALL RIGHTS RESERVED. INTERNATIONAL COPYRIGHT SECURED. B.M.I.

JAMBO

U.A.R.

8, 9, 10

© 1998 BY Mel Bay PUBLICATIONS, INC., PACIFIC, MO 63069.
ALL RIGHTS RESERVED. INTERNATIONAL COPYRIGHT SECURED. B.M.I.

KISS ME

U.A.R.

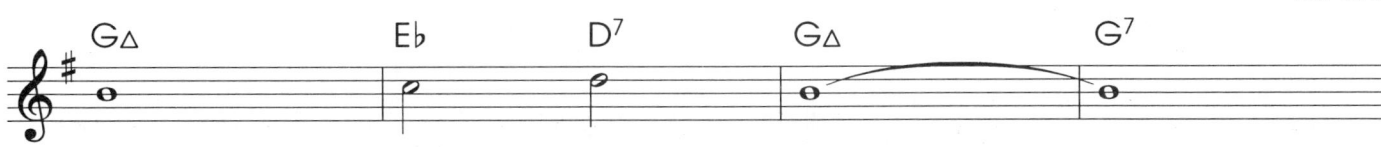
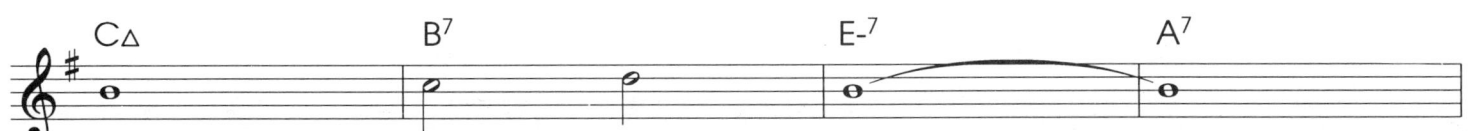
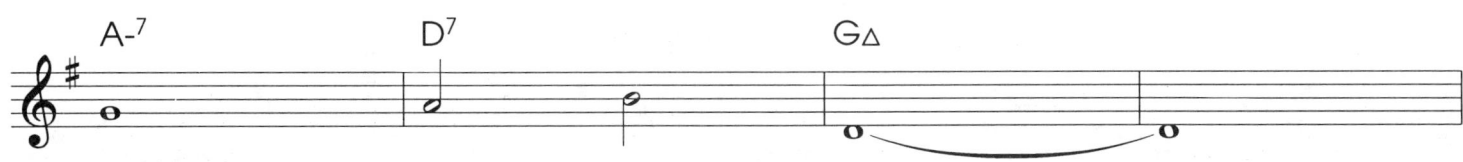
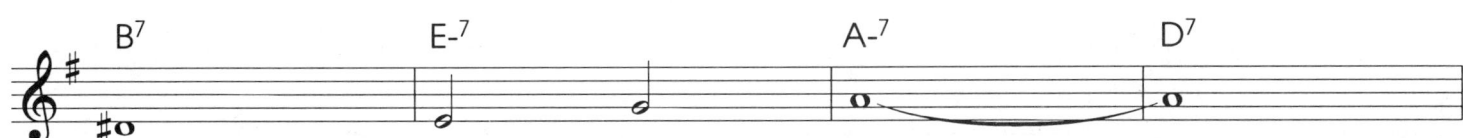
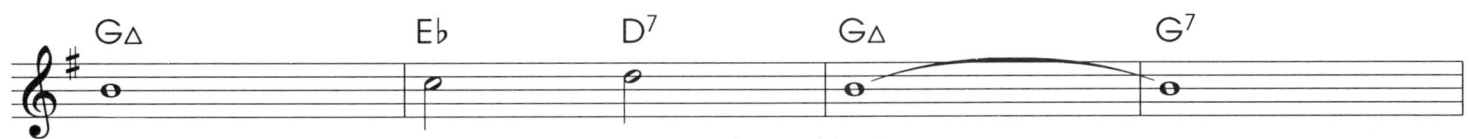
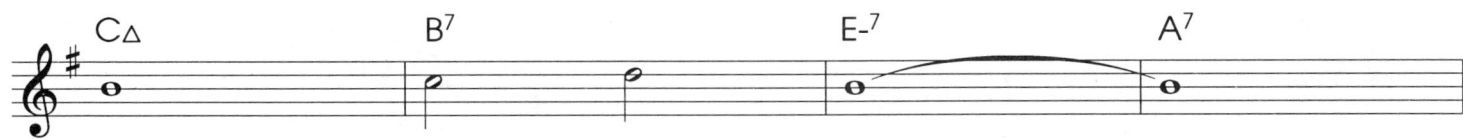
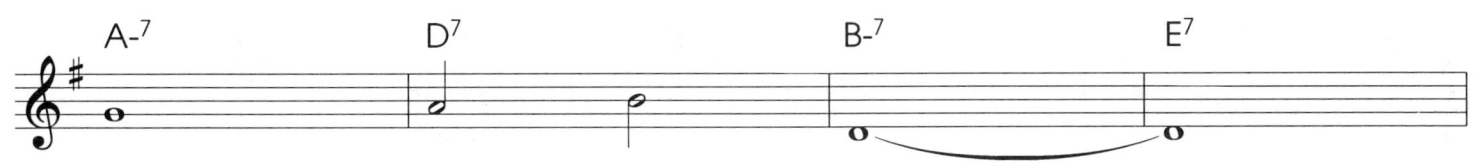

6, 24, 25

© 1998 BY MEL BAY PUBLICATIONS, INC., PACIFIC, MO 63069.
ALL RIGHTS RESERVED. INTERNATIONAL COPYRIGHT SECURED. B.M.I.

NAMORADA

U.A.R.

32, 33

© 1998 BY MEL BAY PUBLICATIONS, INC., PACIFIC, MO 63069.
ALL RIGHTS RESERVED. INTERNATIONAL COPYRIGHT SECURED. B.M.I.

POP QUIZ

U.A.R.

6, 9, 13, 22

© 1998 BY MEL BAY PUBLICATIONS, INC., PACIFIC, MO 63069.
ALL RIGHTS RESERVED. INTERNATIONAL COPYRIGHT SECURED. B.M.I.

QUARTER OF

U.A.R.

Don't be late

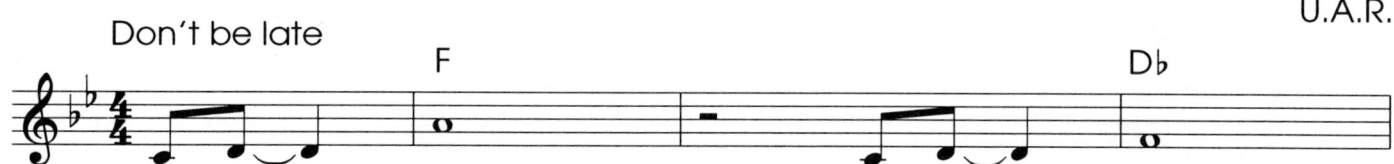
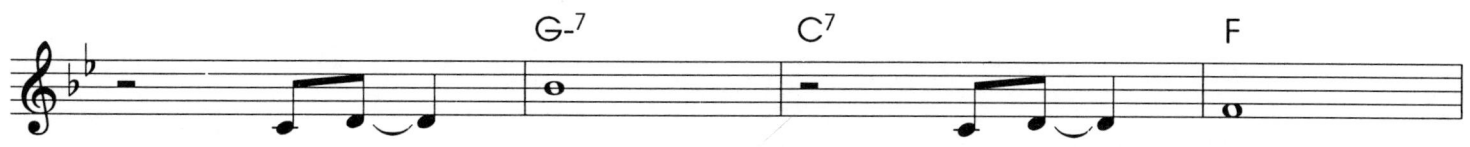
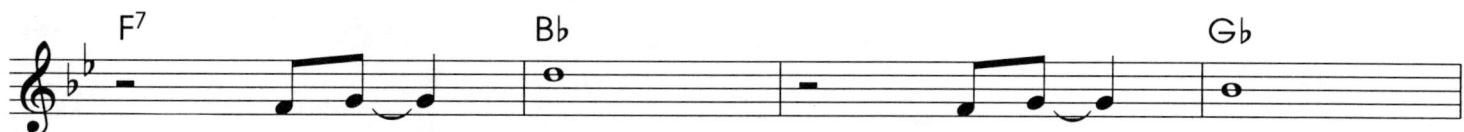

ST. JAMES INFIRMARY

YOU BASKET!

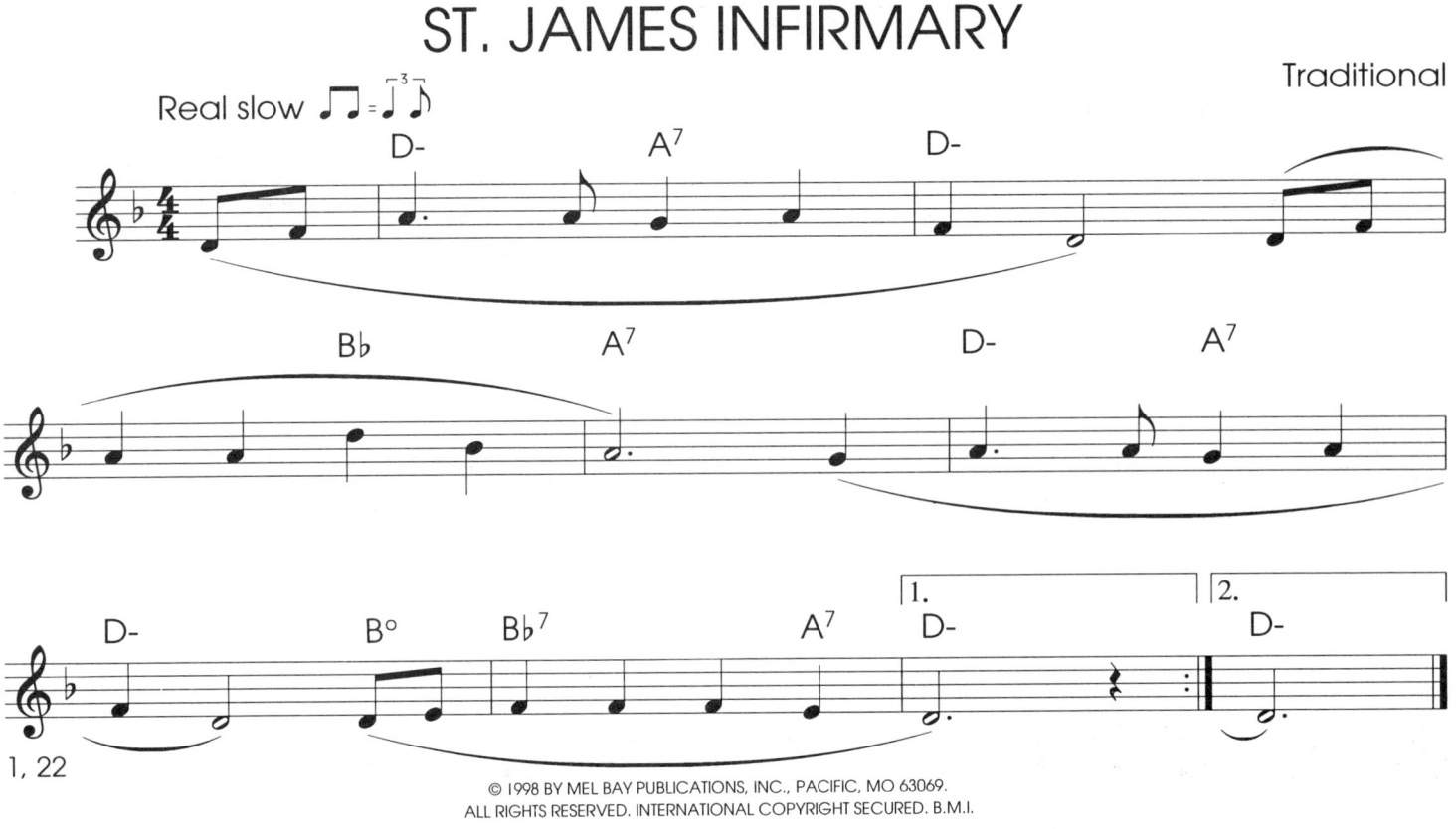

ZAMBEZI

HOW TO SWING

Most of the songs in this book are SWING style. These songs are either marked "swing" at the heading or have the sign: "♫=♩♪".

This means that you should *not* divide the 8th notes of each beat in half evenly, which is standard. Instead, the beats will be divided *unevenly*. The first part of each beat will last longer than the second part.

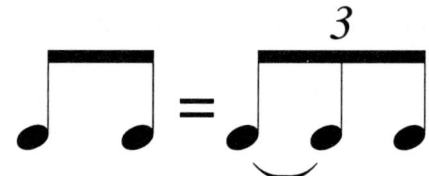

So if it is written:

it will be played:

The "ON THE BEAT" 8th note will last for 2/3 of the beat. The "OFF THE BEAT" 8th note will last 1/3 of the beat.

The direction to "swing" a song affects the whole song. It will be heard in all the 8th notes, and in any accompaniment. Directions like: "funky", "rock beat" or "♫=♫" tells you that the 8th notes are to be played evenly.

Listening to the recording that accompanies this book helps to clarify this rhythm.

SONGBOOK

SESAME RAG

Uri Ayn Rovner

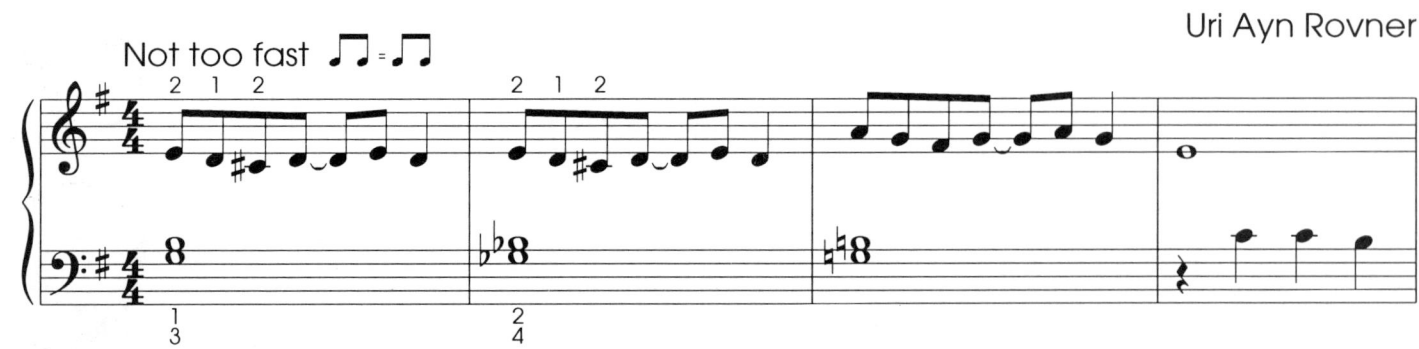

© 1998 BY MEL BAY PUBLICATIONS, INC., PACIFIC, MO 63069.
ALL RIGHTS RESERVED. INTERNATIONAL COPYRIGHT SECURED. B.M.I.

HIGHWAY 1

Uri Ayn Rovner

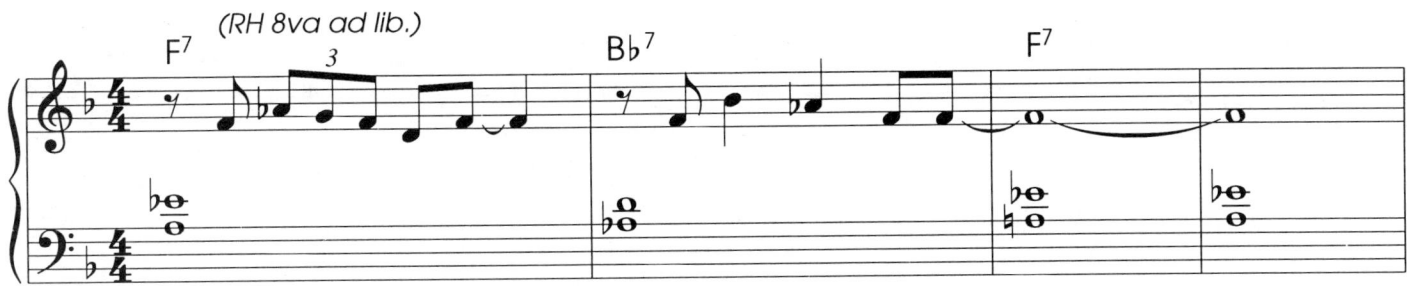

© 1998 BY MEL BAY PUBLICATIONS, INC., PACIFIC, MO 63069.
ALL RIGHTS RESERVED. INTERNATIONAL COPYRIGHT SECURED. B.M.I.

MISS TUREE

Uri Ayn Rovner

SOMETHING DOING

S. Joplin & S. Haydn
Arr. U.A.R.

KAPLOOEY LOUEY

Uri Ayn Rovner

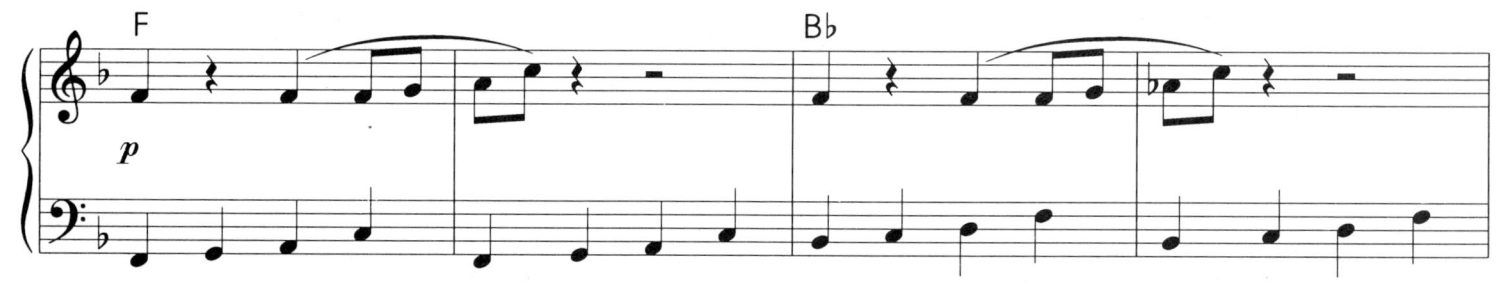

© 1998 BY Mel Bay PUBLICATIONS, INC., PACIFIC, MO 63069.
ALL RIGHTS RESERVED. INTERNATIONAL COPYRIGHT SECURED. B.M.I.

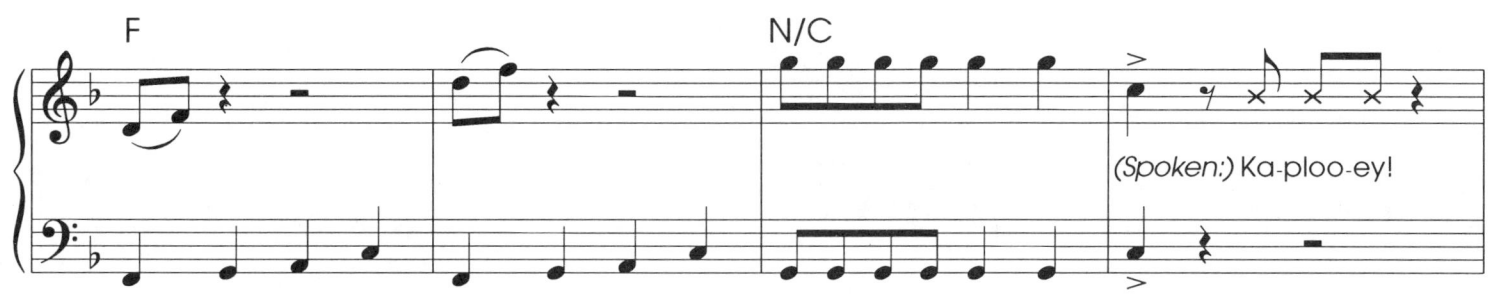
(Spoken:) Ka-ploo-ey!
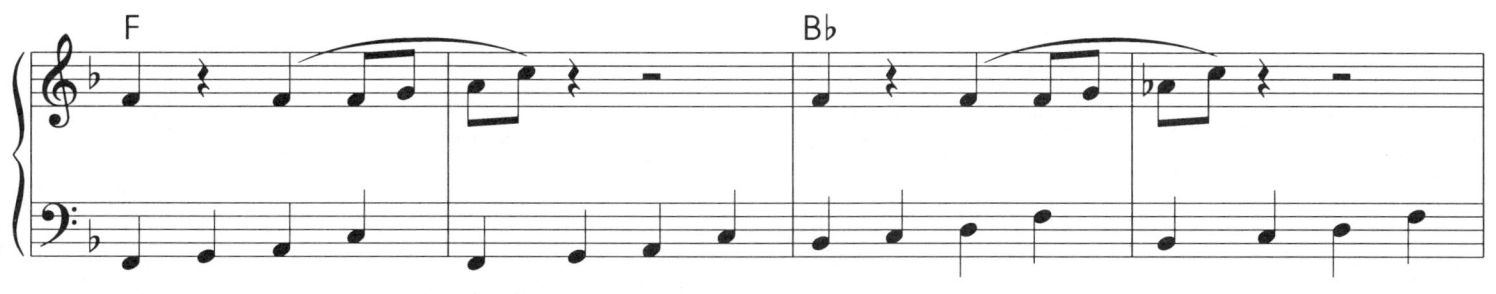

ONE TWO THREE

Uri Ayn Rovner

© 1998 BY MEL BAY PUBLICATIONS, INC., PACIFIC, MO 63069.
ALL RIGHTS RESERVED. INTERNATIONAL COPYRIGHT SECURED. B.M.I.

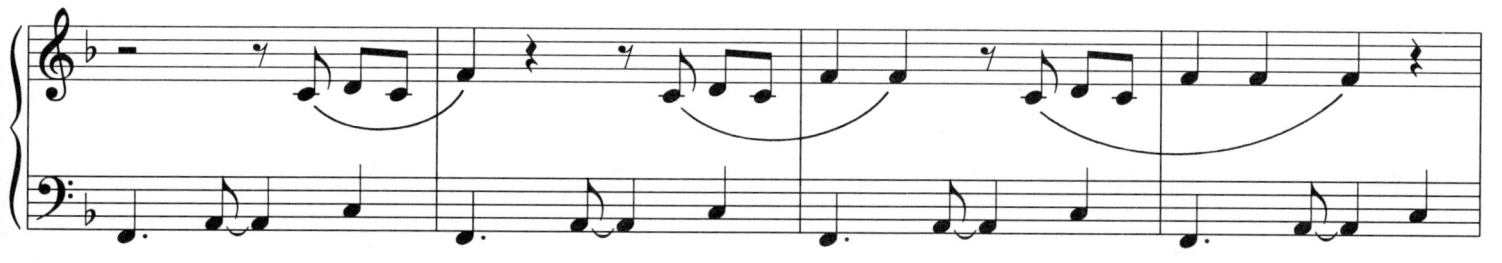

FLAP JACKS

Uri Ayn Rovner

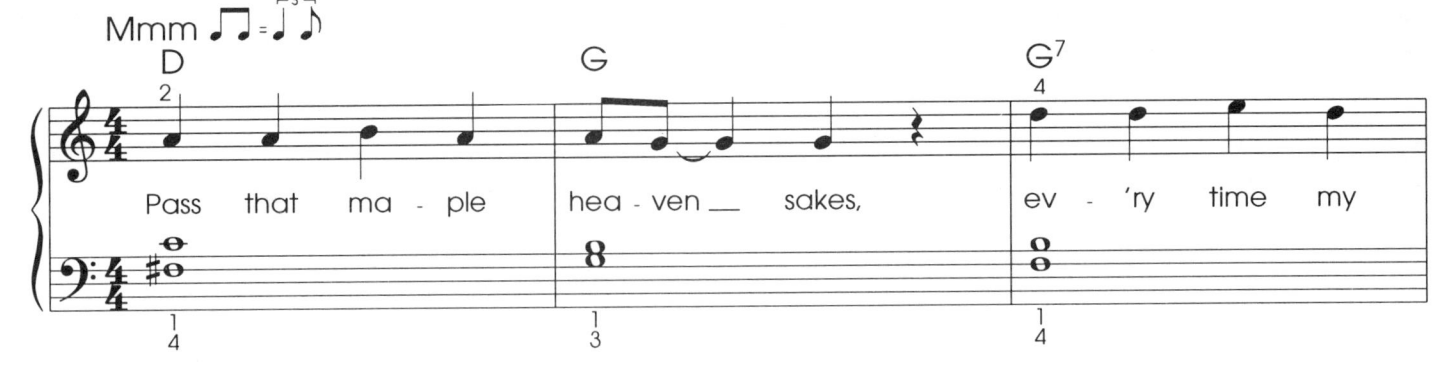
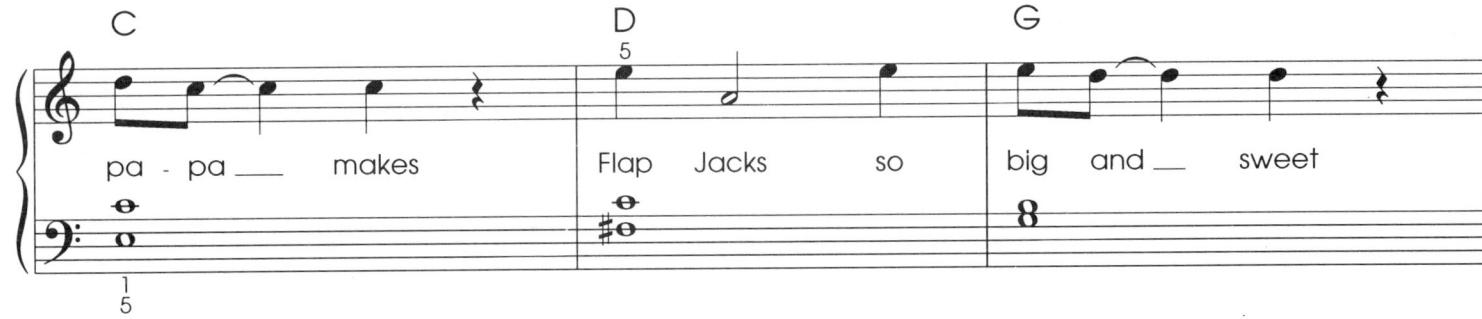

ELITE SYNCOPATIONS

S. Joplin
Arr. U.A.R.

SALLY MANDER

Uri Ayn Rovner

BORNEO BAY
(A JAZZ WALTZ)

Uri Ayn Rovner

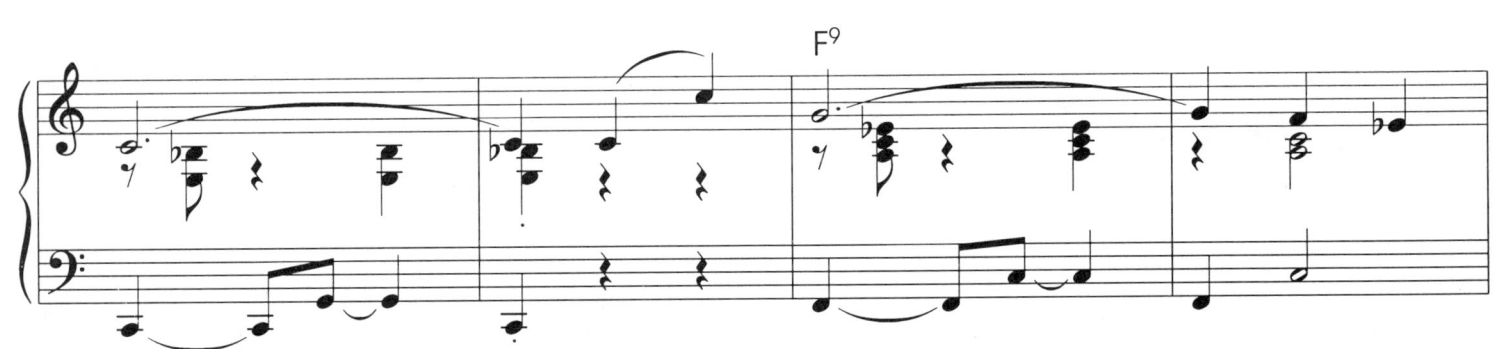

©1995 BY MEL BAY PUBLICATIONS, INC., PACIFIC, MO 63069.
ALL RIGHTS RESERVED. INTERNATIONAL COPYRIGHT SECURED. B.M.I. MADE AND PRINTED IN U.S.A.

POWDER ROOM RAG

Uri Ayn Rovner

CHOC'LATE CAKE

Uri Ayn Rovner

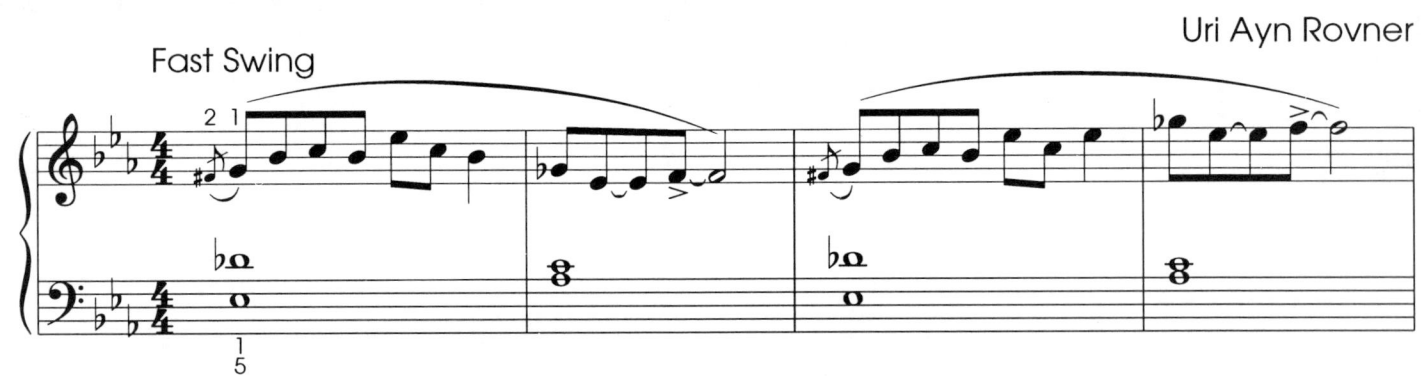

© 1998 BY MEL BAY PUBLICATIONS, INC., PACIFIC, MO 63069.
ALL RIGHTS RESERVED. INTERNATIONAL COPYRIGHT SECURED. B.M.I.

HONG KONG FAREWELL

Uri Ayn Rovner

87

MOONLIGHT IN YOUR EYES

Uri Ayn Rovner

LAST TRAIN TO EDISON

Uri Ayn Rovner

THE HESITATING BLUES

W.C.Handy
Arr. Uri Ayn Rovner

Moderate swing

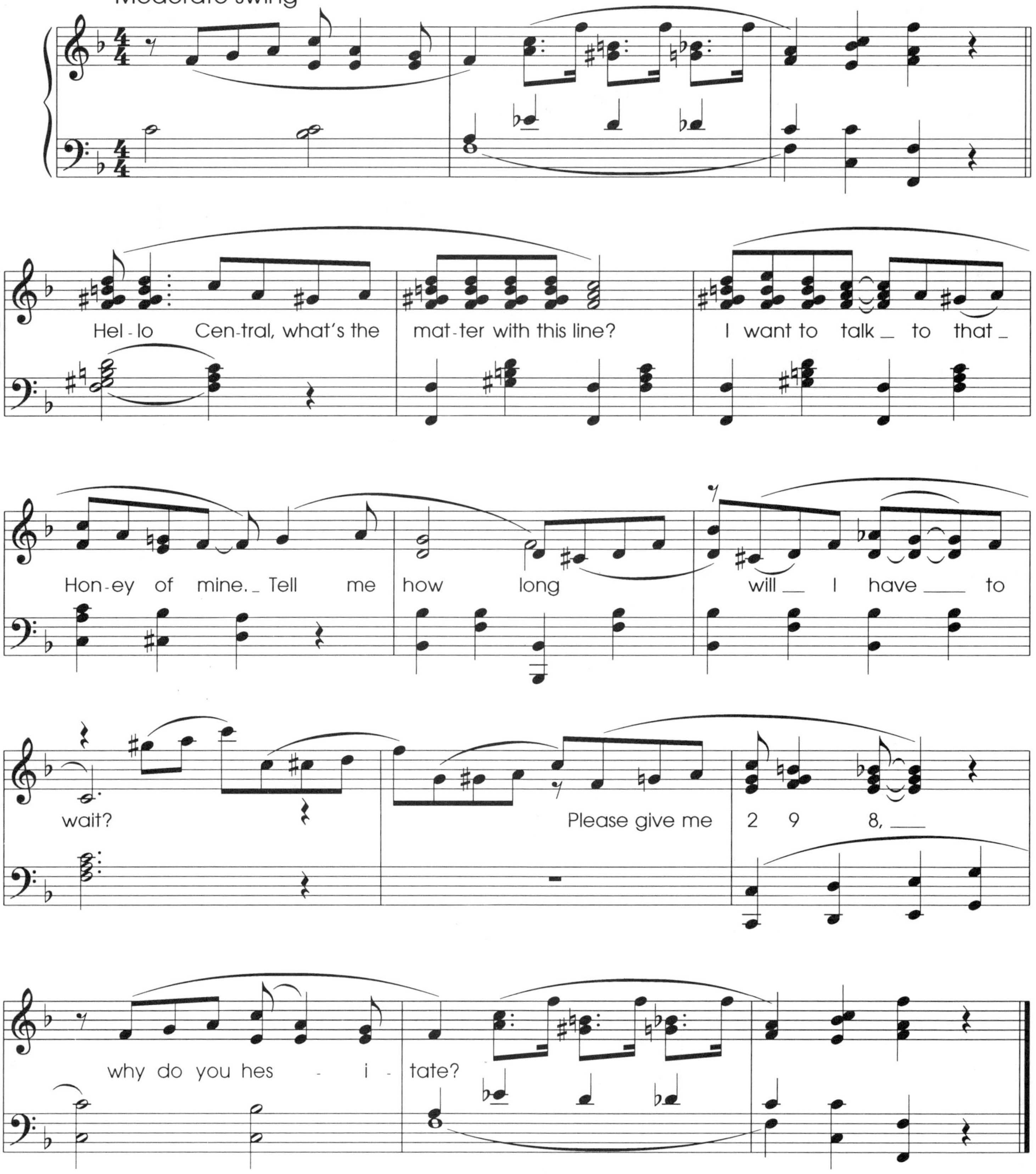

© 1995 BY MEL BAY PUBLICATIONS, INC., PACIFIC, MO 63069
ALL RIGHTS RESERVED. INTERNATIONAL COPYRIGHT SECURED. B.M.I. MADE AND PRINTED IN U.S.A.

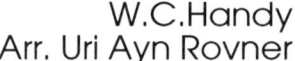

JUST LIKE BEFORE

Uri Ayn Rovner

MANITOULIN

Uri Ayn Rovner

SLAP JACK

Uri Ayn Rovner

FIVER

Uri Ayn Rovner

* + o = 5 beats

© 1998 BY MEL BAY PUBLICATIONS, INC., PACIFIC, MO 63069.
ALL RIGHTS RESERVED. INTERNATIONAL COPYRIGHT SECURED. B.M.I.

The HAPPY DEE HOMEMAKER SHOW

Uri Ayn Rovner

MARACA

Uri Ayn Rovner

YOU'RE WRONG
(Piano Solo)

Uri Ayn Rovner

YOU'RE WRONG
(Piano/Vocal)

Uri Ayn Rovner

FIESTA

Uri Ayn Rovner

Brassy (not fast)

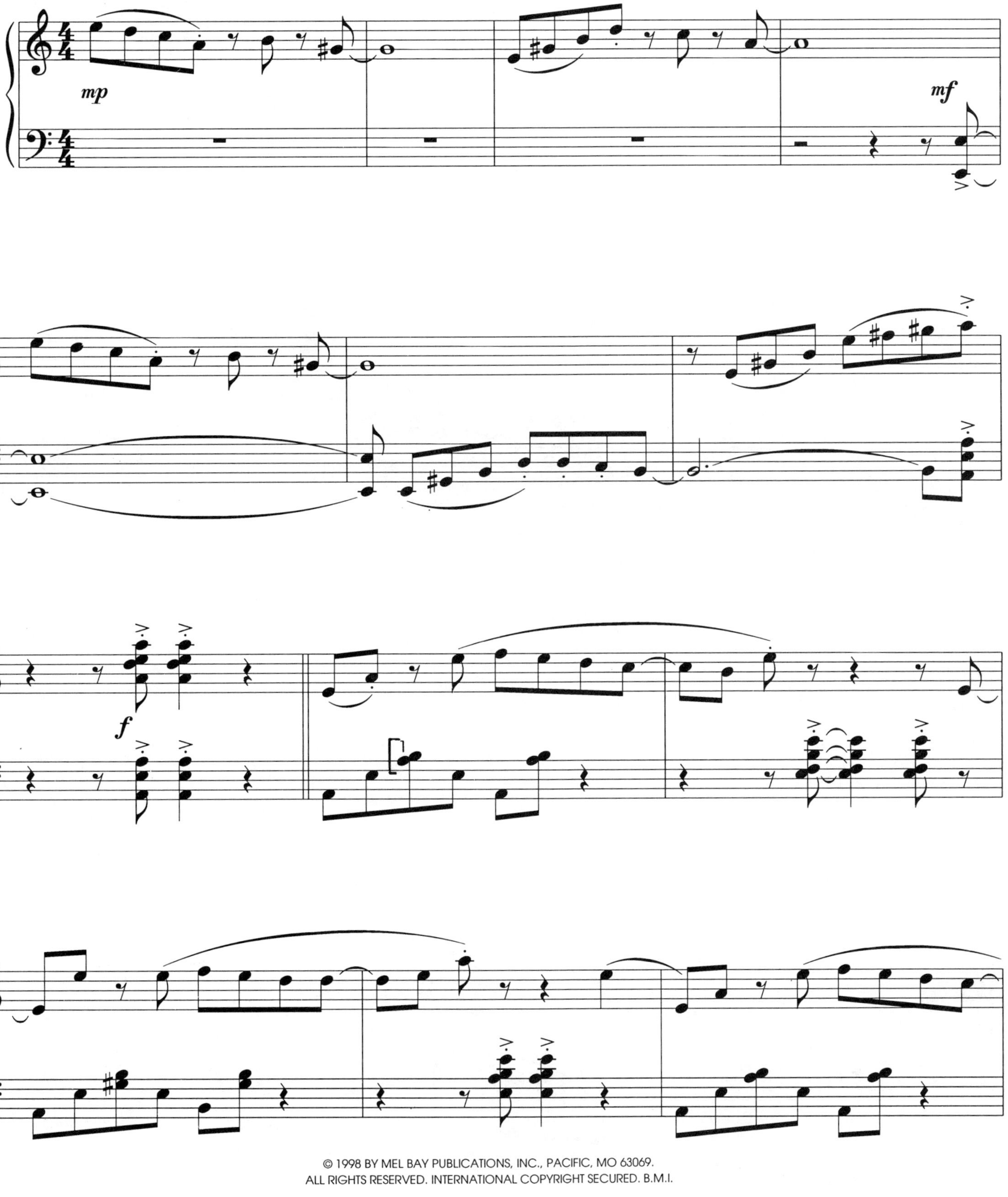

© 1998 BY MEL BAY PUBLICATIONS, INC., PACIFIC, MO 63069.
ALL RIGHTS RESERVED. INTERNATIONAL COPYRIGHT SECURED. B.M.I.

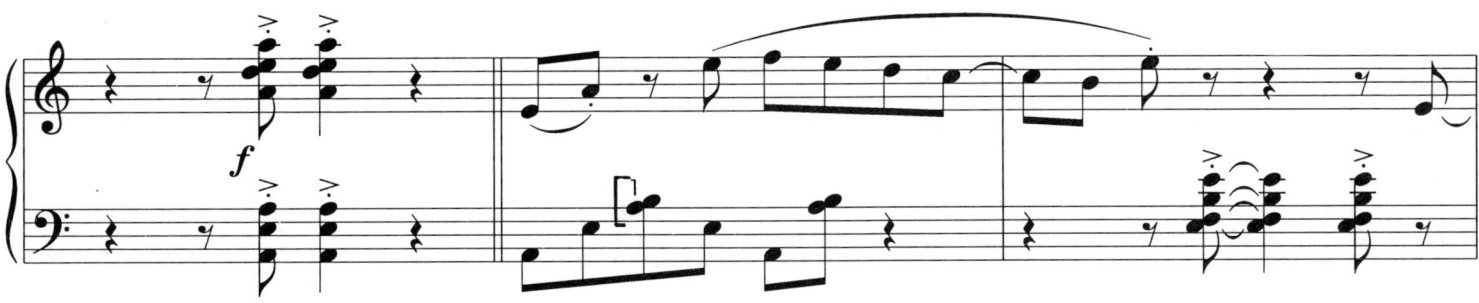

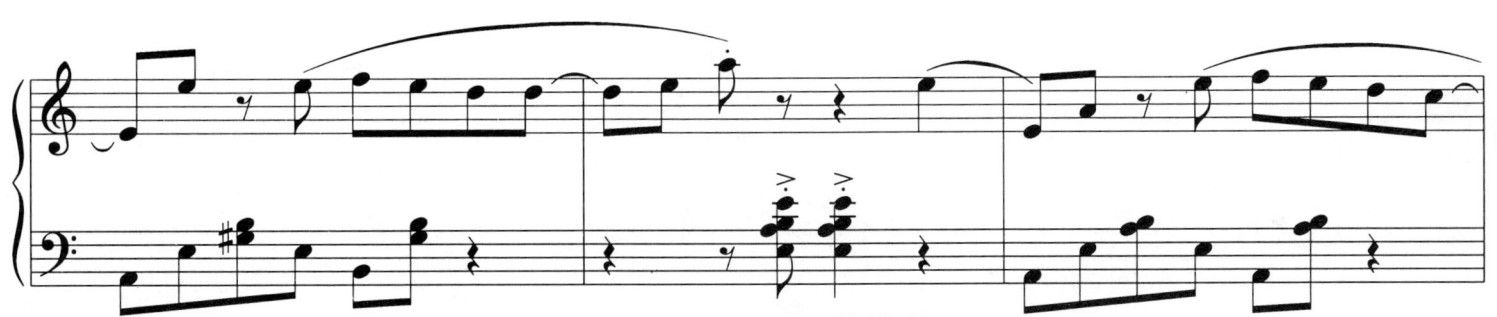

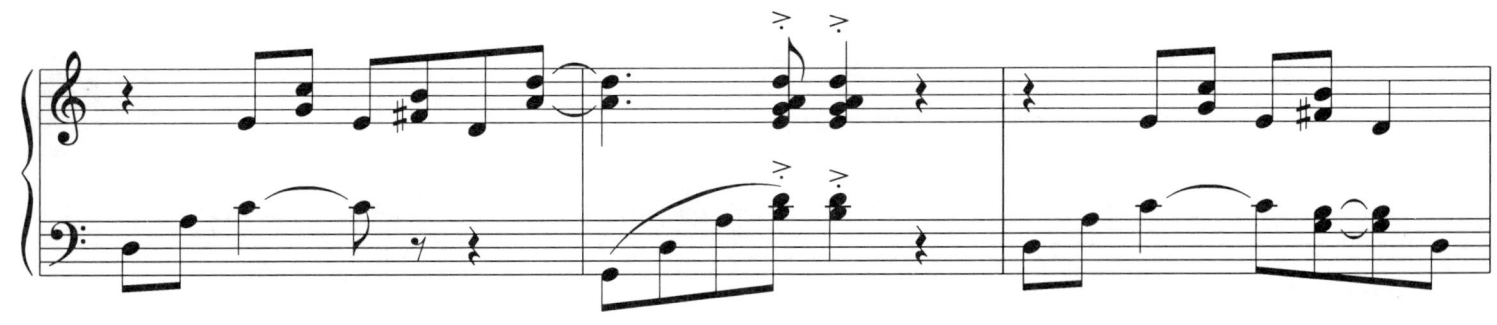

BLUES MONTGOMERY

Uri Ayn Rovner

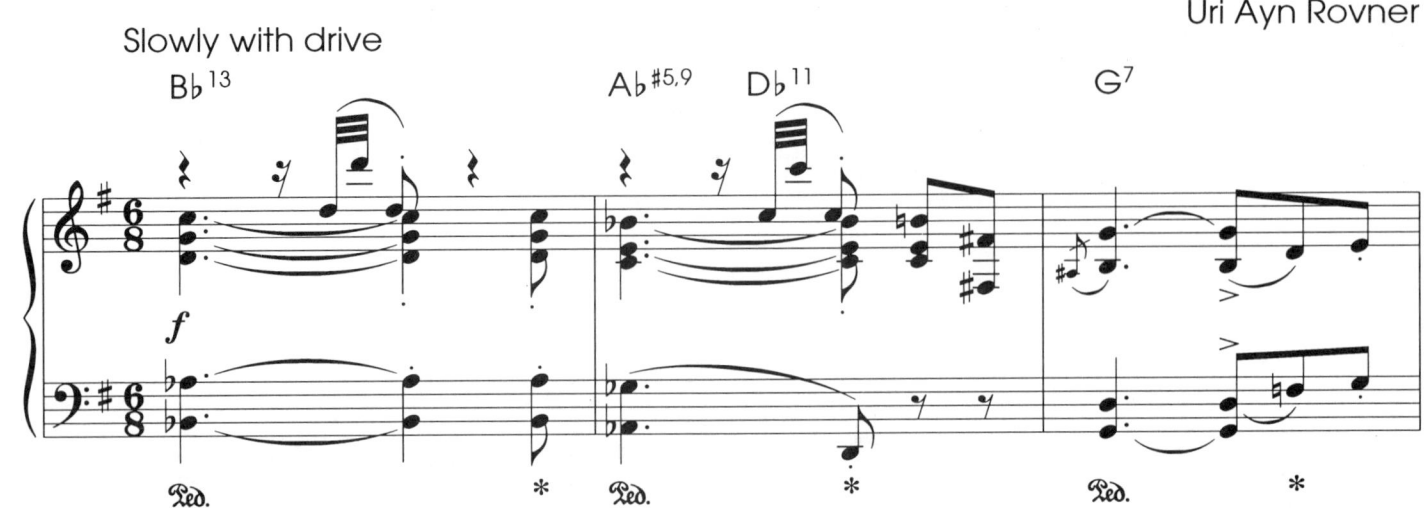

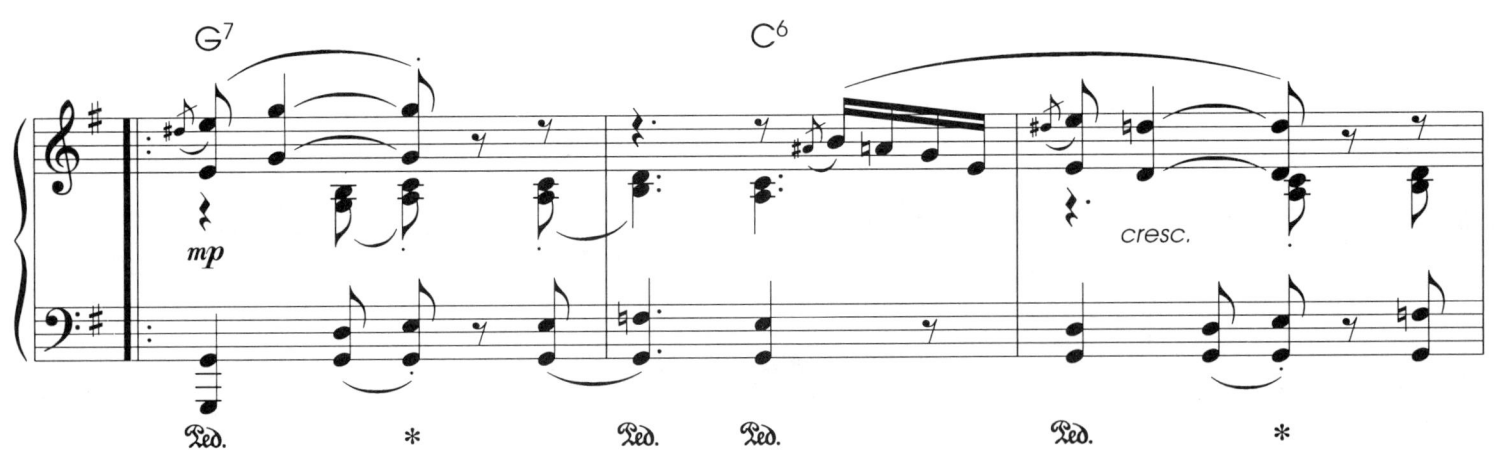

FENDER BENDER

Uri Ayn Rovner